LEARN ALL ABOUT
HOCKEY

® Registered trademark of Hockey Canada
® Marque déposée de Hockey Canada

Officially licensed product of Hockey Canada
Product officiellement licencié de Hockey Canada

The Team Canada logo is a registered trademark of Hockey Canada and is used under license by Fenn/Tundra.
Le logo d'Equipe Canada est une marquee déposée de Hockey Canada et utlisée sous license par Fenn/Tundra.

Published in Canada by Fenn/Tundra of Tundra Books, a division of Random House of Canada Limited,
One Toronto Street, Suite 300, Toronto, Ontario M5C 2V6

Published in the United States by Fenn/Tundra of Tundra Books of Northern New York,
P.O. Box 1030, Plattsburgh, New York 12901

Library of Congress Control Number: 2012937511

Library and Archives Canada Cataloguing in Publication

Huberts, Al
Hockey Canada's learn all about hockey : coloring and activity /
by Al Huberts ; illustrated by Frank Bailey.

ISBN 978-1-77049-436-7

1. Hockey – Juvenile literature. 2. Coloring books – Juvenile literature.
I. Bailey Frank, 1956- II. Title.

GV847.25.H83 2012   j796.962   C2012-902540-2

We acknowledge the financial support of the Government of Canada through the Canada Book Fund and that of the
Government of Ontario through the Ontario Media Development Corporation's Ontario Book Initiative. We further
acknowledge the support of the Canada Council for the Arts and the Ontario Arts Council for our publishing program.

www.tundrabooks.com

Printed and bound in the United States of America

1 2 3 4 5 6   17 16 15 14 13 12

RULE 1 COLOR-IT ™

LEARN ALL ABOUT HOCKEY

COLORING

AND

ACTIVITY BOOK

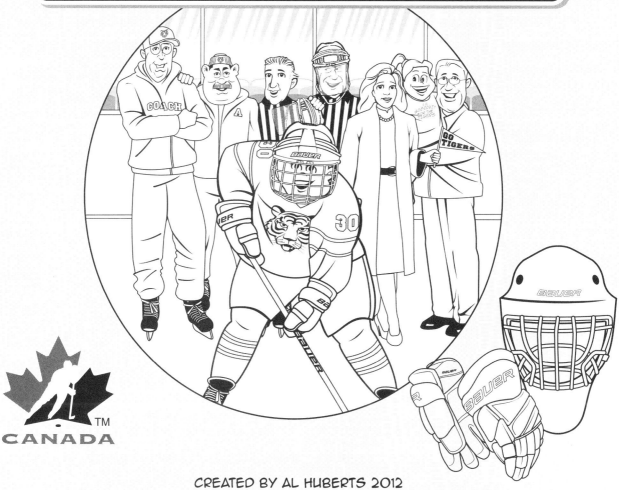

CANADA ™

CREATED BY AL HUBERTS 2012
ILLUSTRATED BY FRANK BAILEY

The Smith family stops at the Blueline Diner
on their way to the arena.

The Smith family arrives for hockey
practice prepared and on time.

3

TIGERS' FIRST LINE

9   MORETTI
LEFT WING

12   ERIKSSON
LEFT DEFENSE

22   O'REILLY
RIGHT WING   Ⓐ

6   SANDERS
RIGHT DEFENSE

30   SMITH
CENTER   Ⓒ

1   DEVRIES
GOALIE

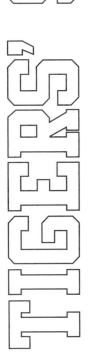

15 BECKER
RIGHT WING

28 O'SULLIVAN
LEFT DEFENSE

21 GARCIA
LEFT WING

23 SINGH
RIGHT DEFENSE

4 BURE
CENTER

2 JONES
GOALIE

31 **BINDA**
LEFT WING

24 **PERRAULT**
LEFT DEFENSE

19 **VANDERBY**
RIGHT WING

5 **LUI**
RIGHT DEFENSE

33 **COLLINS**
CENTER

COACH EVANS

ASSISTANT COACH
MOREAU

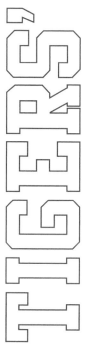

7

8

The Tigers get dressed in league-approved equipment.

TEAM

9

SPOT THE DIFFERENCES

Can you spot the **twenty** differences between
this drawing and the one on pages 8 and 9?

MUSTANGS

MUSTANGS' FIRST LINE

18 HAVEL
LEFT WING

26 WALKER
LEFT DEFENSE

7 SCHRODER Ⓒ
RIGHT WING

23 MOORE
RIGHT DEFENSE

31 LOPEZ Ⓐ
CENTER

8 TAYLOR
GOALIE

MUSTANGS' SECOND LINE

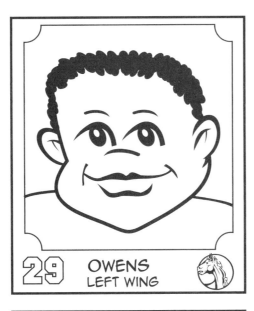

29 OWENS
LEFT WING

14 BIANCHI
LEFT DEFENSE

16 MACDONALD
RIGHT WING

11 MENARD
RIGHT DEFENSE

10 O'CONNER
CENTER

17 LAINE
GOALIE

MUSTANGS' THIRD LINE

32 JANNSEN
LEFT WING

27 BOWER
LEFT DEFENSE

25 MILLER
RIGHT WING

34 ROBINSON
RIGHT DEFENSE

20 HOWE
CENTER

COACH MURPHY

ASSISTANT COACH
CASSIDY

VISI

The Mustangs get dressed in league-approved equipment.
Can you find **ten** hockey sticks on these two pages?

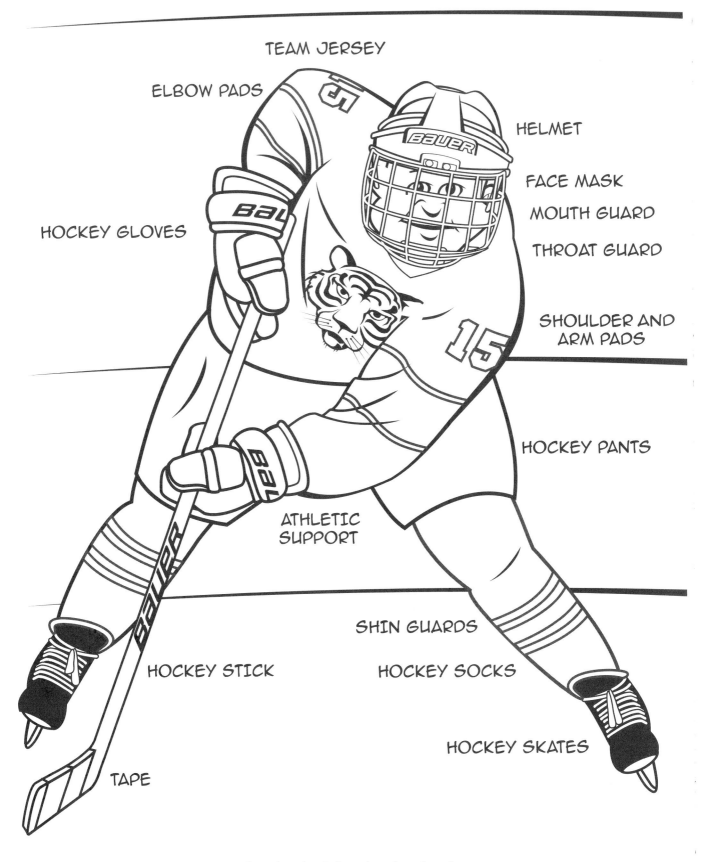

TEAM JERSEY

ELBOW PADS

HELMET

FACE MASK

MOUTH GUARD

THROAT GUARD

HOCKEY GLOVES

SHOULDER AND
ARM PADS

HOCKEY PANTS

ATHLETIC
SUPPORT

SHIN GUARDS

HOCKEY STICK

HOCKEY SOCKS

HOCKEY SKATES

TAPE

Becker (#15), right wing for the Tigers,
is fully dressed in **league-approved equipment**.

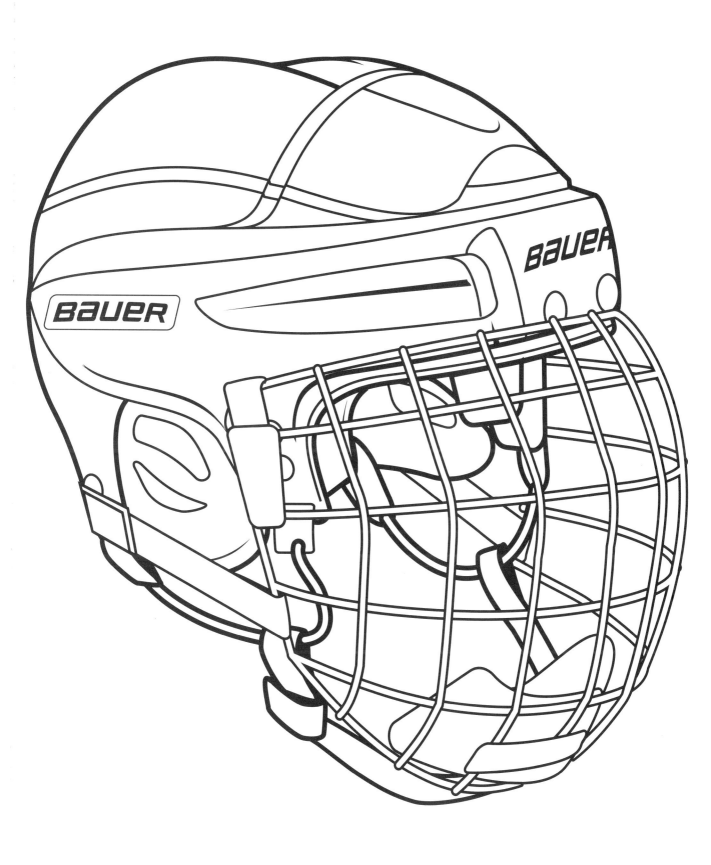

HOCKEY HELMET

19

HOCKEY SKATES

HOCKEY GLOVES

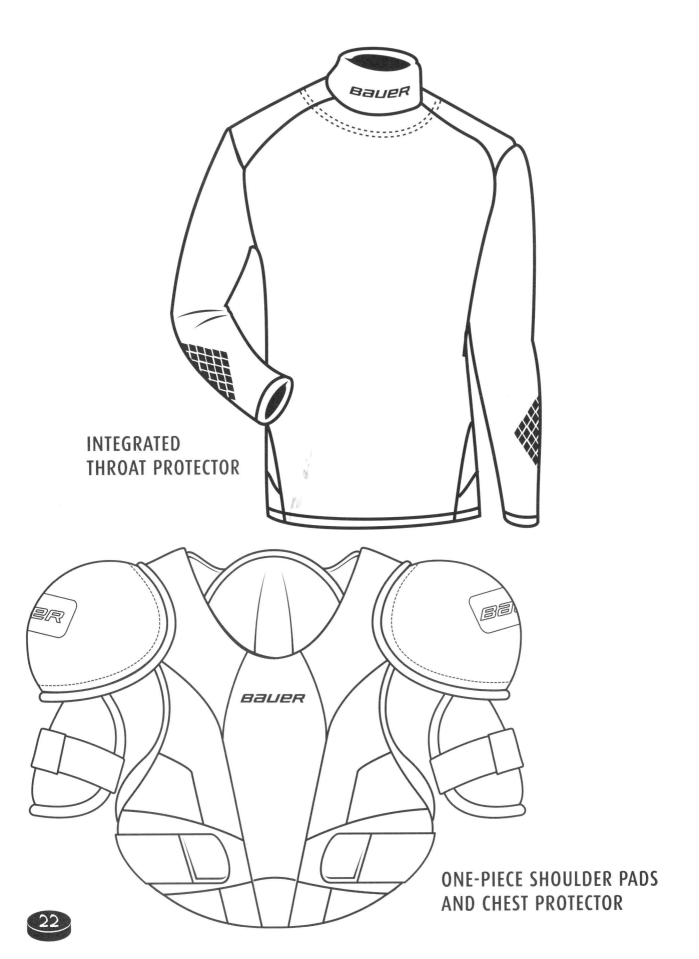

INTEGRATED
THROAT PROTECTOR

ONE-PIECE SHOULDER PADS
AND CHEST PROTECTOR

22

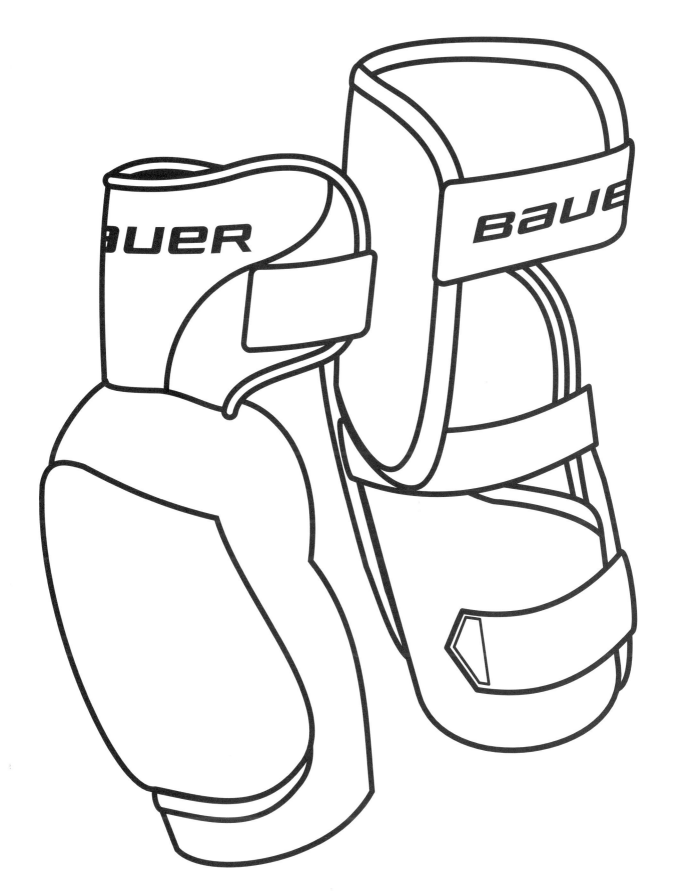

ELBOW PADS

23

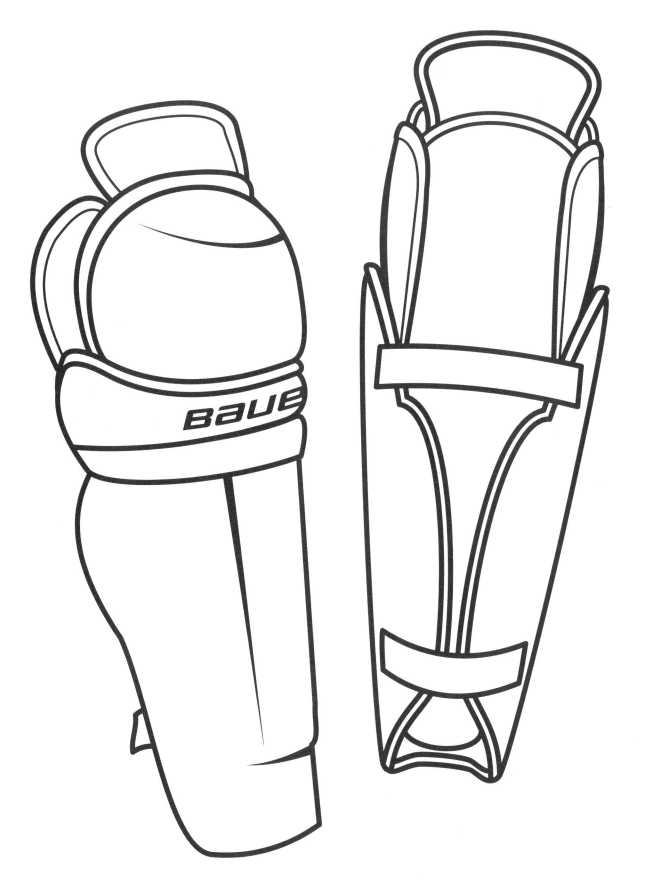

SHIN PADS

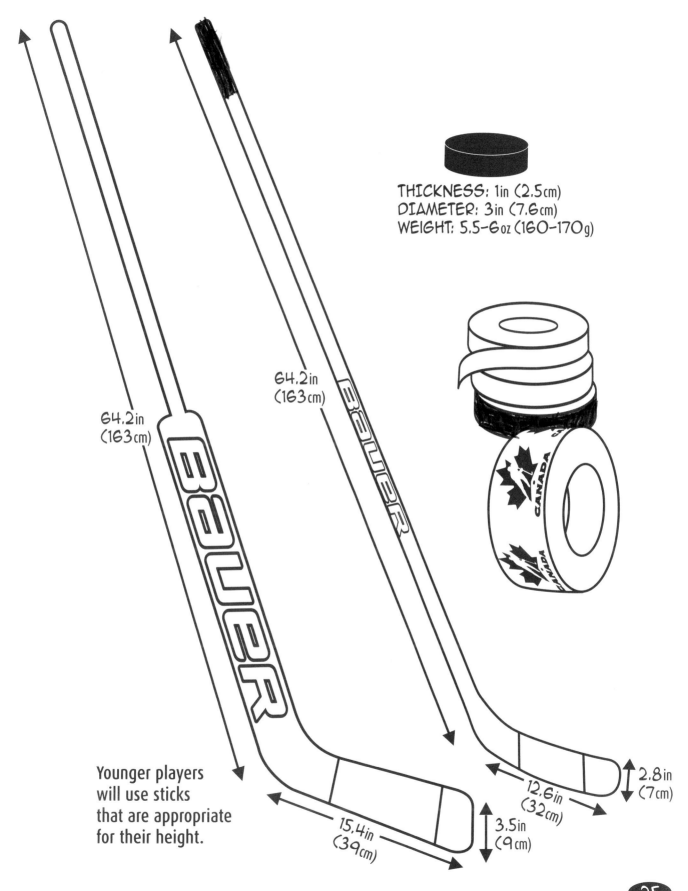

THICKNESS: 1in (2.5cm)
DIAMETER: 3in (7.6cm)
WEIGHT: 5.5–6oz (160–170g)

64.2in
(163cm)

64.2in
(163cm)

64.2in
(163cm)

Younger players
will use sticks
that are appropriate
for their height.

2.8in
(7cm)

12.6in
(32cm)

3.5in
(9cm)

15.4in
(39cm)

HOCKEY STICKS, PUCK, AND TAPE.

25

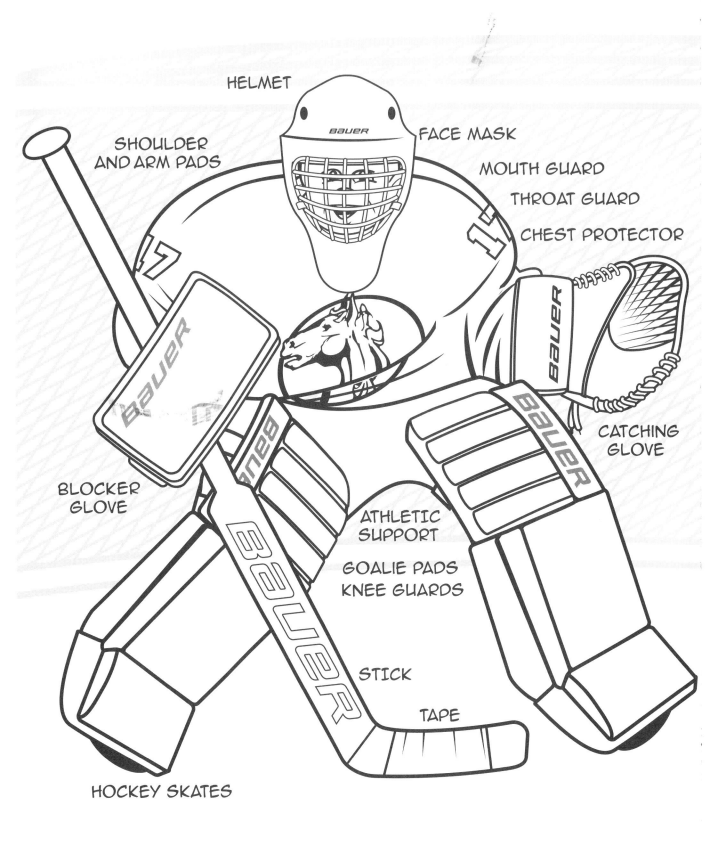

HELMET

SHOULDER
AND ARM PADS

FACE MASK

MOUTH GUARD

THROAT GUARD

CHEST PROTECTOR

CATCHING
GLOVE

BLOCKER
GLOVE

ATHLETIC
SUPPORT

GOALIE PADS
KNEE GUARDS

STICK

TAPE

HOCKEY SKATES

Laine (#17), goalie for the Mustangs,
is fully dressed in **league-approved equipment**.

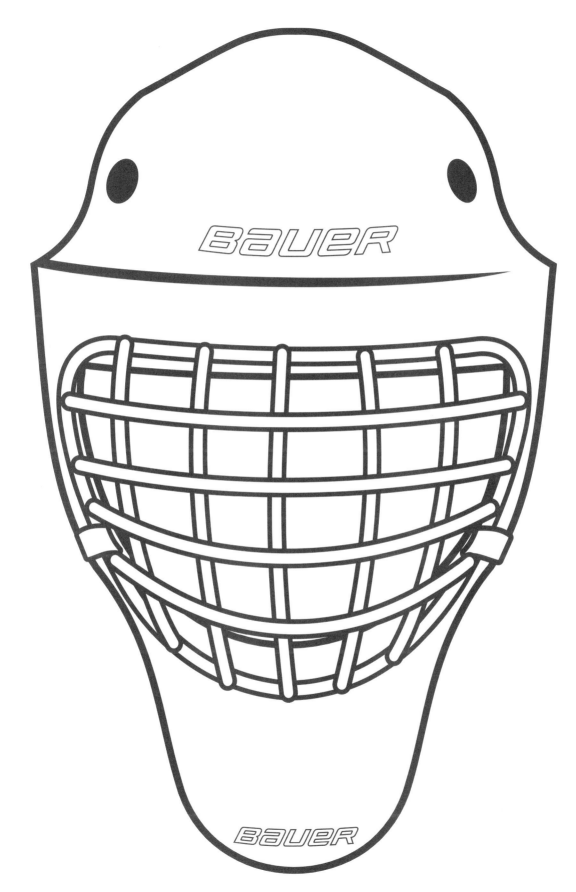

Design your own goalie mask.

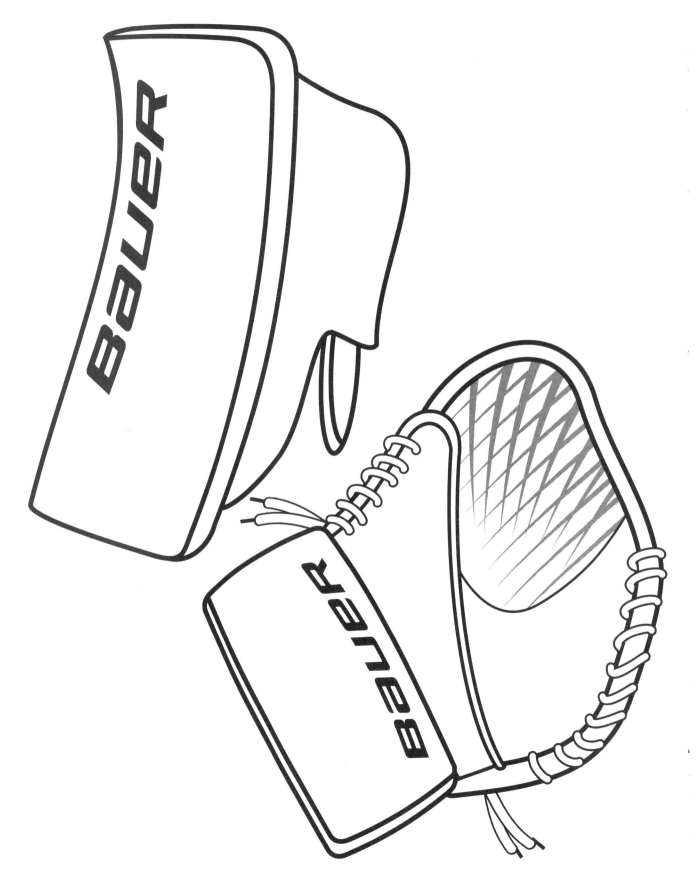

GOALIE BLOCKER AND CATCHER

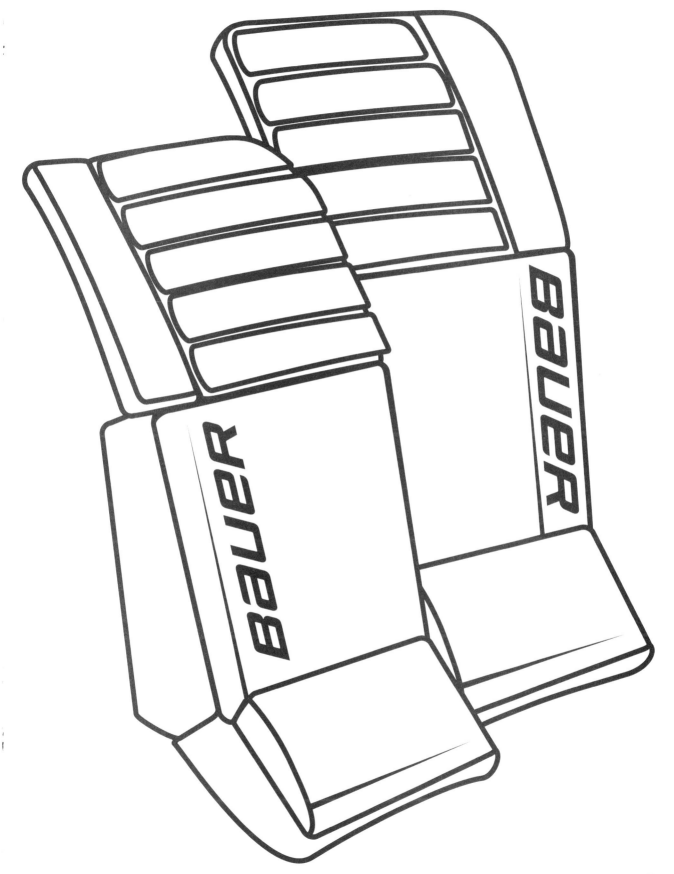

GOALIE PADS

EQUIPMENT WORD SEARCH

```
H U K C U P A T E N
O G S B L A D E S E
C A A O L A O T T G
K M M A P O T A E K
E E E R A A C S M A
Y C C D N P T K L U
B L A S T C A A E A
A O F T S T P T H R
G C G L O V E E A C
A K N I R N Q S R A
```

SKATES	PUCK	HELMET
PANTS	FACE MASK	GLOVE
RINK	BLOCKER	TAPE
HOCKEY BAG	BLADES	NET
GAME CLOCK	BOARDS	

Can you find the names of the different
pieces of hockey equipment?

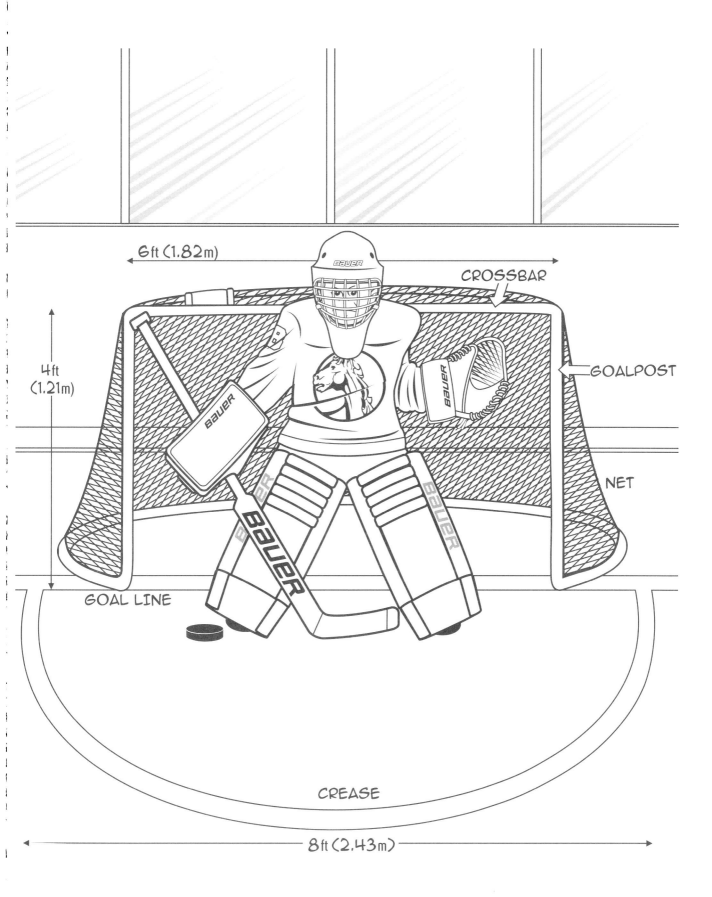

6ft (1.82m)

CROSSBAR

4ft (1.21m)

GOALPOST

NET

GOAL LINE

CREASE

8ft (2.43m)

Taylor (#8), goalie for the Mustangs,
takes his position in front of the net.

OFFICIAL ICE HOCKEY SURFACE

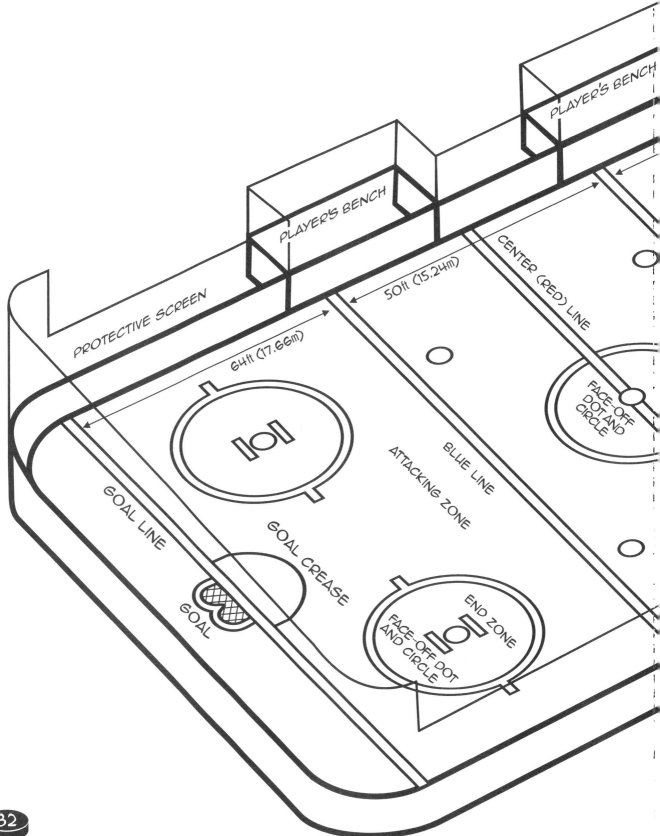

PLAYER'S BENCH

PLAYER'S BENCH

PROTECTIVE SCREEN

50ft (15.24m)

CENTER (RED) LINE

64ft (17.66m)

FACE-OFF DOT AND CIRCLE

BLUE LINE

ATTACKING ZONE

GOAL LINE

GOAL CREASE

END ZONE

FACE-OFF DOT AND CIRCLE

GOAL

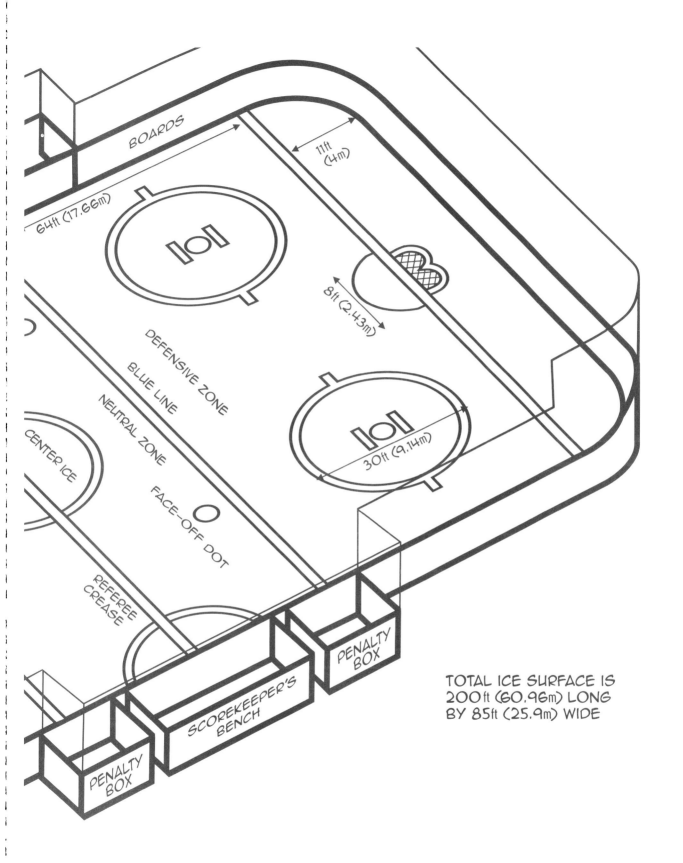

BOARDS

64ft (17.66m)

11ft (4m)

8ft (2.43m)

30ft (9.14m)

DEFENSIVE ZONE

BLUE LINE

NEUTRAL ZONE

CENTER ICE

FACE-OFF DOT

REFEREE CREASE

PENALTY BOX

SCOREKEEPER'S BENCH

PENALTY BOX

TOTAL ICE SURFACE IS 200ft (60.96m) LONG BY 85ft (25.9m) WIDE

These are the key elements and measurements of a hockey rink.

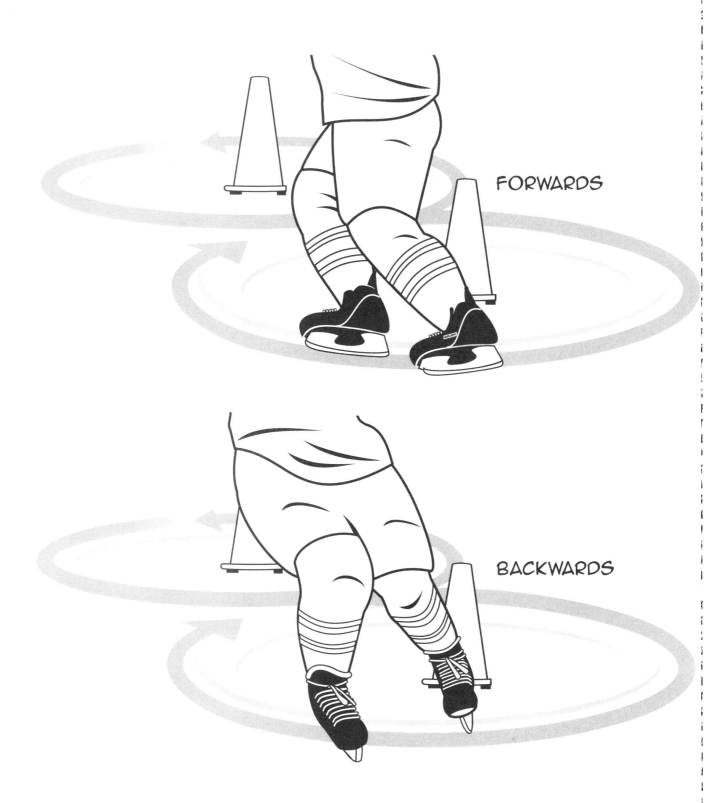

FORWARDS

BACKWARDS

It takes a lot of practice
to become a good skater.

 34

A good hockey player must have
strong **stick** and **puck-handling skills**.

At practice, Tigers' coaches Evans and Moreau take
the players through a **skating drill**.

SKATE MAZE

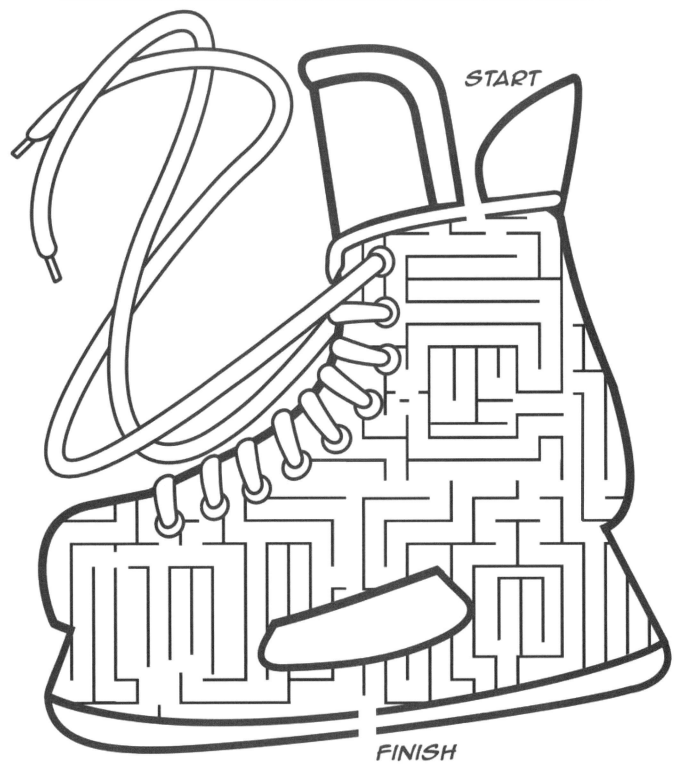

START

FINISH

Travel from the top of the skate to the blade.

MATCH THE DESCRIPTION TO THE CORRECT HOCKEY TERM

____ BREAKAWAY   ____ BLOCKED SHOT   ____ BLIND PASS

____ BOARDS   ____ ASSIST   ____ BENCH MINOR

____ BACKHAND   ____ BODYCHECK   ____ BLUE LINE

____ BACKCHECK   ____ BLOCKER   ____ ATTACKING ZONE

DESCRIPTION

1. The point awarded to a player who makes a pass that sets up a goal.

2. The area between the opposing team's blue line and goal line.

3. When forwards check the opposing team's player(s) while skating back to their defensive zone.

4. To pass the puck without looking.

5. The twelve-inch parallel lines that run across the ice and divide the neutral zone from the offensive and defensive zones.

6. The forty-two-inch-high (1.06m) wall around a hockey rink that is topped with safety glass.

7. When a player bumps an opposing player that is either in control of the puck or has just passed the puck.

8. A shot that is stopped by a defending player before it reaches the goaltender.

9. When an attacking player carries the puck by the opposing defensemen and skates in alone on the goalie.

10. The large padded glove used by goalies to block shots and hold their hockey stick.

11. A penalty given to a team, usually for an infraction by the coach, such as too many players on the ice.

12. A shot or pass using the backside of the hockey stick blade.

GAME 1

39

At practice, Mustangs' coaches Murphy and Cassidy take the players through a **star passing drill**.

 42

At practice, Tigers' coaches Evans and Moreau take
the players through a **horseshoe shooting drill**.

MUSTANGS'
ATTACKING ZONE   NEUTRAL ZONE   MUSTANGS'
DEFENSIVE ZONE

TIGERS' DEFENSIVE ZONE   TIGERS' ATTACKING ZONE

The Tigers' and Mustangs' players line up for
a **face-off** in the Mustangs' defensive zone.

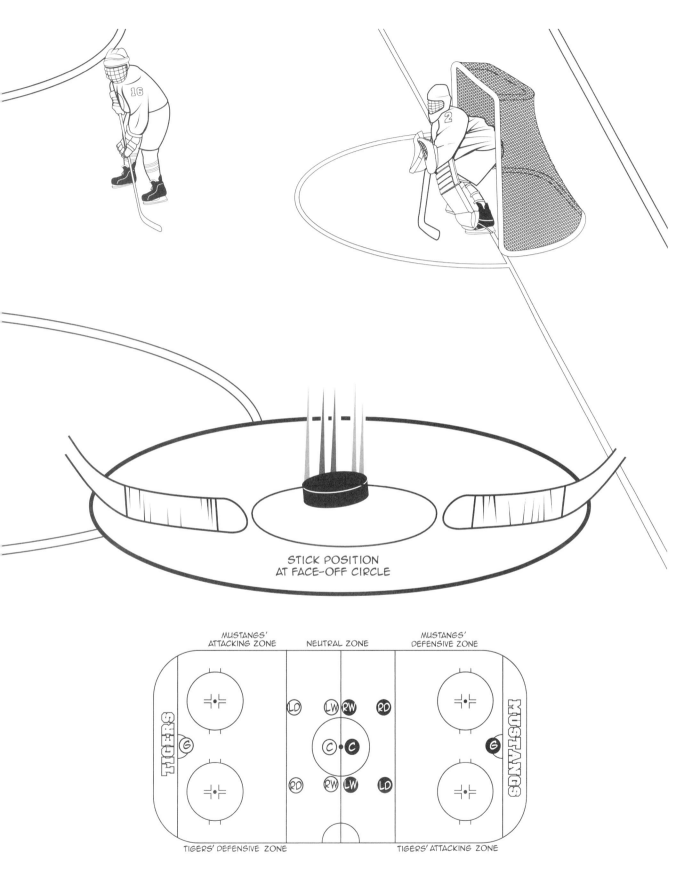

STICK POSITION
AT FACE-OFF CIRCLE

MUSTANGS'
ATTACKING ZONE

NEUTRAL ZONE

MUSTANGS'
DEFENSIVE ZONE

TIGERS

MUSTANGS

TIGERS' DEFENSIVE ZONE

TIGERS' ATTACKING ZONE

The lineup for a **face-off** at center ice.

Vanderby (#19), right wing for the Tigers,
is caught **offside** on this play. He crossed into
the attacking zone ahead of the puck.

STOP

OFFSIDE

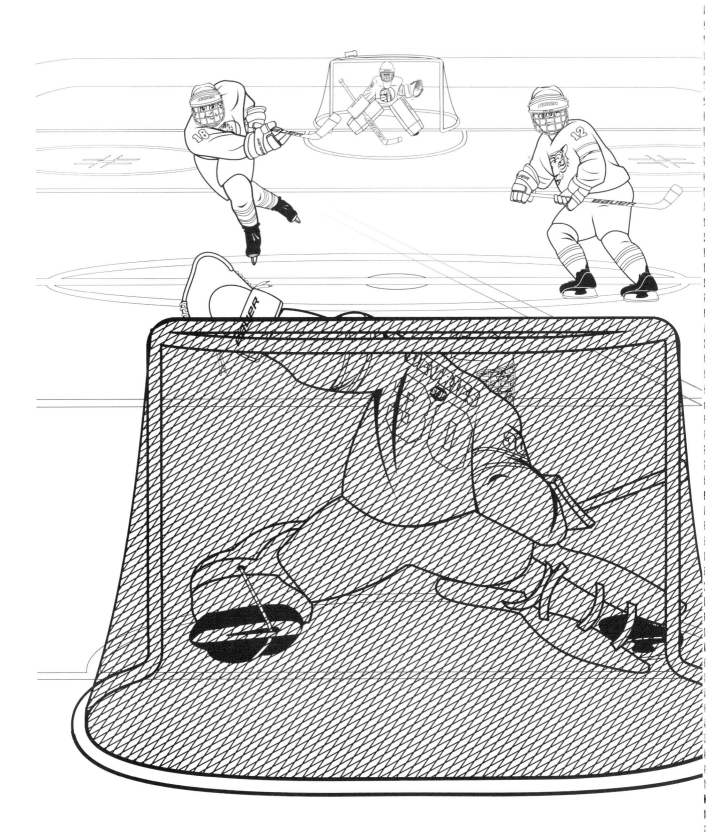

 Havel (#18), left wing for the Mustangs,
ices the puck.

ICING

49

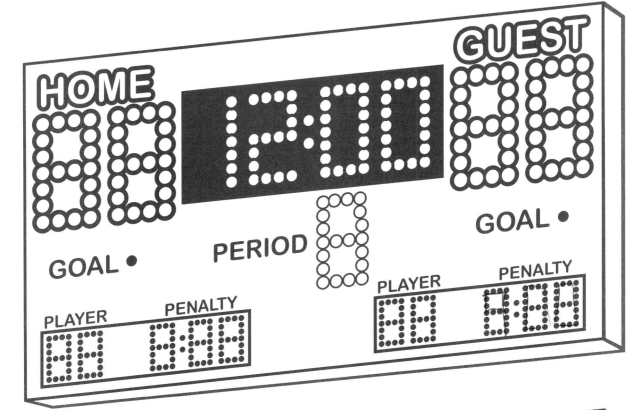

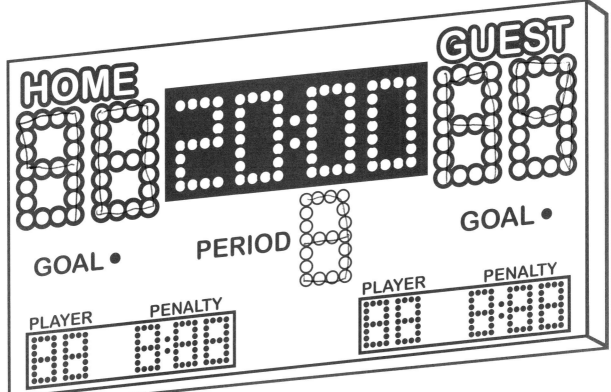

The length of each period depends
on the age of the players.

_____ CREASE   _____ CENTER ICE   _____ CLEARING THE PUCK

_____ CENTER   _____ CATCHER   _____ FACE-OFF CIRCLE

_____ CHECK   _____ CENTERING   _____ CHANGE ON THE FLY

_____ BOX   _____ CENTER LINE   _____ BREAKAWAY PASS

DESCRIPTION

1. A pass to a teammate who is trying for a breakaway.

2. A defensive alignment used by a team to defend against a power play.

3. The glove that a goalie uses to catch the puck.

4. The player in the middle of the forward line that usually leads their team's attack and takes part in most face-offs.

5. The area between the two blue lines; also referred to as the neutral zone.

6. The twelve-inch-wide (30.5cm) red line that runs across the ice halfway between the two goals.

7. A pass towards the middle of the ice surface to a teammate that has a better shot on net.

8. The thirty-foot (9.14m) circle at the center of the ice surface where the puck is dropped to start the game and to restart the game after a goal is scored.

9. When players on the bench replace those on the ice while play is in progress.

10. The semicircle area in front of the goal that protects the goalie from attacking players.

11. When contact is made by a defending player against an opposing player to get the puck away from them or to slow them down.

12. When a player shoots the puck out from in front of their net or their defensive zone.

GAME 2

The Tigers' coach calls a **time-out** to discuss important strategy at a key point in the game.

Line changes ensure players are rested for their shifts.

SPOT THE DIFFERENCES
Can you spot the **ten** differences between
this drawing and the one on page 54?

HOCKEY EQUIPMENT CROSSWORD

ACROSS

5. NEEDED TO MOVE ALONG THE ICE
6. USED BY PLAYERS TO CONTROL AND SHOOT THE PUCK
7. PROTECTS A PLAYER'S HANDS
8. PROTECTS A JOINT AT THE CENTER OF A PLAYER'S ARM
10. PROTECTS THE LOWER FRONT OF A PLAYER'S LEGS
11. PROTECTS A PLAYER'S MOUTH
13. OFFICIAL HOCKEY EQUIPMENT SUPPLIER
14. USED BY A GOALIE TO BLOCK PUCKS

DOWN

1. PROTECTS A PLAYER'S UPPER BODY
2. PROTECTS A PLAYER'S HEAD FROM INJURIES
3. USED BY THE GOALIE TO GRAB THE PUCK
4. IT IS 1in (2.5)cm X 3in (7.6cm)
7. PROTECTS A GOALIE'S FACE
9. PROTECTS A PLAYER'S EYES
12. PROTECTS A GOALIE'S LEGS

Schroder (#7), right wing for the Mustangs,
makes a **backhand pass** to his left wing
teammate, Havel (#18).

HOCKEY ARENA TERMS CROSSWORD

ACROSS
1. THEY SURROUND THE PLAYING SURFACE
7. THERE ARE FIVE OF THEM
9. THE LINE THAT CROSSES THE ICE SURFACE BETWEEN THE GOAL LINE AND THE CENTER LINE
11. THE RED LINE BETWEEN THE GOALPOSTS
12. THE ZONE NEAREST A TEAM'S GOAL THAT IS BEING DEFENDED
13. THE TWO LINES THAT EXTEND FROM THE FACE-OFF CIRCLE
14. THE AREA IN FRONT OF THE GOAL WHERE A GOALIE CAN PLAY UNOBSTRUCTED
15. THE MATERIAL THAT SURROUNDS THE GOAL

DOWN
2. THE AREA BETWEEN THE OPPOSING TEAM'S BLUE LINE AND GOAL LINE
3. WHERE PLAYERS WITH A PENALTY SIT
4. THE AREA BETWEEN THE BLUE LINES
5. THE FROZEN SURFACE THAT THE GAME IS PLAYED ON
6. THE DOT AT THE CENTER OF THE FACE-OFF CIRCLE
8. THE SEMICIRCLE IN FRONT OF THE TIMEKEEPER'S BENCH
10. WHERE PLAYERS SIT WHEN NOT ON THE ICE

Miller (#25), right wing for the Mustangs,
takes a **wrist shot** towards the Tigers' goal.

59

O'Reilly (#22), right wing for the Tigers, winds up
and takes a **slapshot**. The puck is coming fast and hard!

Smith (#30), center for the Tigers, makes a
forehand pass to his left wing teammate, Moretti (#9).

61

 62

Schroder (#7), right wing for the Mustangs,
makes a **drop pass** to his center teammate, Lopez (#31).

PEOPLE
WORD SEARCH

```
E N D R A W R O F T
T I R E Y A L P A R
N A L E F T W I N G
A T I O T E A M S N
T P N F S E N E Z I
S A E A T T C S H W
I C S C O A C H E T
S E M R O S T E R H
S R E N I A R T T G
A I N G O A L I E I
H O M E T E A M A R
```

COACH	PLAYER	ROSTER
FORWARD	LEFT WING	RIGHT WING
GOALIE	DEFENSE	FANS
LINESMEN	ASSISTANT	CAPTAIN
TEAMS	HOME TEAM	TRAINER

Can you find the names of the different people
and players who participate in hockey?

Lui (#5), defenseman for the Tigers,
makes a **lead pass** to where left wing
Binda (#31) will be in a few seconds.

_____ CROSSBAR   _____ COVER   _____ DEFENSIVE ZONE

_____ DEKE THE GOALIE _____ DELAY OF GAME _____ CLEARING THE ZONE

_____ CROSS-CHECK   _____ DEFENSIVE LINE _____ DEAD PUCK

_____ DEFENSEMEN   _____ DEFLECTION   _____ DELAYED CALL

DESCRIPTION

1. A puck that is shot out of the rink or that a player catches and holds in his hand.

2. The players who make up the defensive line, usually positioned in or near the defensive zone, to help the goalie guard against the opposing team.

3. The zone nearest a team's goal that they are defending.

4. When the puck hits a stick or skate and goes into the net or when a goalie hits the puck away.

5. A fake motion or move by the puck carrier to confuse the opposing goalie.

6. The horizontal bar that connects the top of the two goalposts.

7. When an official raises their arm to call a penalty on one team, but does not blow the whistle until the play by the opposing team is completed.

8. When a player deliberately causes a stoppage in play by dislodging the goalpost or by shooting the puck out of the rink.

9. When a player holds their hockey stick with both hands and drives the shaft into an opposing player.

10. When an attacking player skates out of the defensive zone to avoid being called offside when a teammate carries or passes the puck back into the zone.

11. When a player shadows an opposing player to stop them from receiving a pass or making an offensive play.

12. The two players that make up a team's defensive unit, usually positioned in or near the defensive zone.

GAME 3

 66

Jannsen (#32), left wing for the Mustangs,
makes a **centering pass** to teammate
Howe (#20), in front of the Tigers' net.

Lui (#5), defenseman for the Tigers, uses a
flip pass to get the puck over the stick
of Howe (#20), center for the Mustangs.

Bianchi (#14), defenseman for the Mustangs,
is forced to make a **blind pass** by Singh (#23),
defenseman for the Mustangs.
Who will get the puck?

Becker (#15), right wing for the Tigers, is in the offensive zone which makes his **hand pass** illegal.

ILLEGAL
HAND PASS

 Vanderby (#19), defenseman for the Tigers, makes a
breakaway pass to teammate Collins (#33).

GOALIE MASK MAZE

START

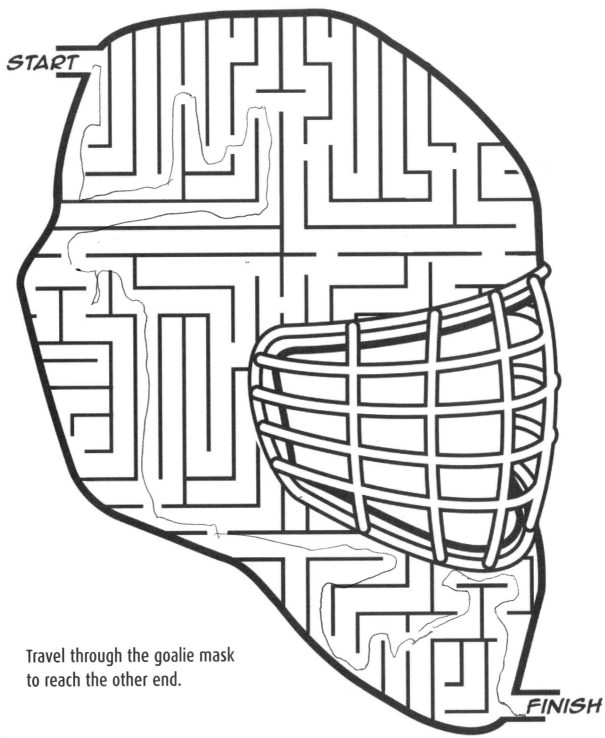

Travel through the goalie mask
to reach the other end.

FINISH

WORD SCRAMBLE #1
A-D

UNSCRAMBLE THE LETTERS AND USE THE CLUE TO FIND THE CORRECT HOCKEY TERM.

TSIISSA	TO HELP	_____
LOCKERB	GOALIE GLOVE	_____
HANDKCAB	OPPOSITE FOREHAND	_____
WAYAKAERB	ON YOUR OWN	_____
HERCATC	GRABS PUCKS	_____
TAINPAC	TEAM LEADER	_____
ENTERC	MIDDLE FORWARD	_____
INGCHARG	TWO-STRIDE PENALTY	_____
KCEHC	TAKE PUCK	_____
ACHCO	TEACHES AND GUIDES	_____
REASEC	GOALIE'S TERRITORY	_____
RABSSORC	BETWEEN THE GOALPOSTS	_____
FENSEDEMEN	STOP FORWARD ATTACKERS	_____
EVID	FAKE INFRACTION	_____
PORD SSAP	LEAVE PUCK BEHIND	_____

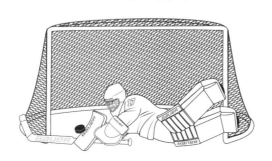

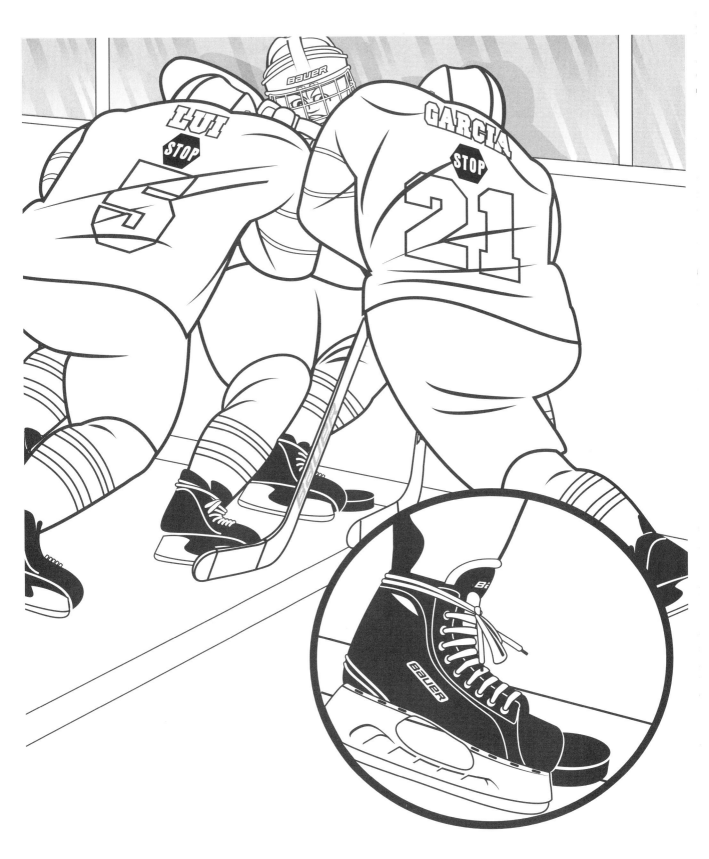

The referee calls a stop in play.
Miller (#25), right wing for the Mustangs,
has **frozen** the puck on the boards.

74

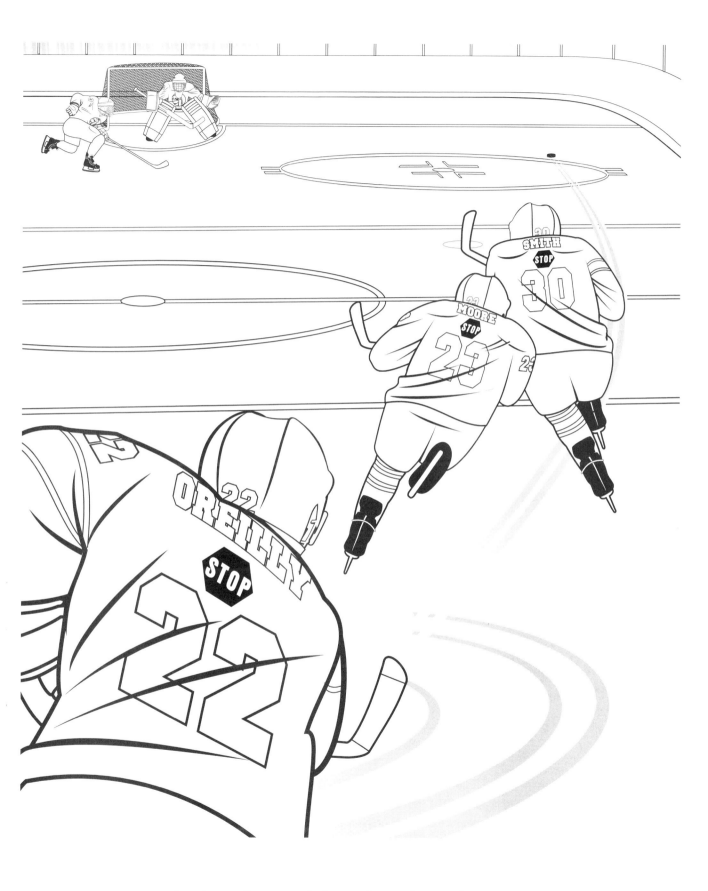

The Tigers **dump and chase** the puck into the corner.
Smith (#30), center for the Tigers, will try to get to it first.

 76 Walker (#26), defenseman for the Mustangs, passes the puck
across the two blue lines to left wing Havel (#18).

The puck crosses two blue lines,
putting Havel **offside**.

OFFSIDE

Schroder (#7), right wing for the Mustangs,
scrambles to get out of the defensive zone to avoid
an offside call. He needs to **clear the zone**.

78

MATCH THE DESCRIPTION TO THE CORRECT HOCKEY TERM

_____ FACE-OFF   _____ ELBOWING   _____ DELAYED OFFSIDE

_____ DROP PASS   _____ DUMP AND CHASE _____ EXTRA ATTACKER

_____ EVEN STRENGTH   _____ DOUBLE MINOR   _____ EMPTY-NET GOAL

_____ HAND PASS   _____ FACE-OFF CIRCLES AND DOTS

DESCRIPTION

1. When an attacking player enters the defensive zone before the puck but the defensive team takes possession of the puck and has an opportunity of bringing the puck out of the defending zone. The referee does not whistle down the play until the attacking team regains possession of the puck.

2. When a puck is moved forward with an open hand in the defensive zone.

3. A penalty given when a player is off the ice for four minutes, during which time no substitutions are permitted.

4. When a player leaves the puck for a teammate following behind.

5. When a team shoots the puck into the attacking zone and chases it in the hope of getting possession of it.

6. When a player strikes an opposing player with their elbow.

7. When a player shoots the puck into the net after the goalie has been pulled.

8. When both teams have the same number of players on the ice.

9. When one team has the advantage of having an extra player on the ice.

10. When the referee drops the puck between the sticks of two opposing players to start each period or to resume play when the game has stopped for other reasons.

11. The one blue and four red circles and spots where face-offs take place.

GAME 4

Collins (#33), center for the Tigers,
backchecks Robinson (#34), defenseman
for the Mustangs.

Lui (#5), defenseman for the Tigers,
poke checks the puck away from
Jannsen (#32), left wing for the Mustangs.

Binda (#31), left wing for the Tigers,
forechecks Howe (#20), center for
the Mustangs.

O'Connor (#10), center for the Mustangs, makes
a **sweep check** to take the puck away
from Garcia (#21), left wing for the Tigers.

Sanders (#6), defenseman for the Tigers, gives a
legal **shoulder check** to Lopez (#31), center for the Mustangs.
Bodychecks are not allowed until players reach a certain age.

84

Menard (#11), defenseman for the Mustangs,
gives a legal **hip check** to Garcia (#21),
left wing for the Tigers.

HOCKEY PERSONNEL CROSSWORD

ACROSS

1. HE OR SHE RUNS THE TEAM FROM THE BENCH
4. THEY CHEER THEIR TEAM
5. THE TEAM LEADER ON THE ICE
7. THEY ARE USED IF A GOAL IS DISPUTED
9. THEY ASSIST THE REFEREE
11. THEY PLAY BETWEEN THE WINGERS
12. THEY PLAY RIGHT OF CENTER
13. A PLAYER THAT EXCELS WHEN THEIR TEAM IS SHORTHANDED
14. THE HEAD OFFICIAL ON THE ICE
15. THEY WORK WITH THE PLAYERS TO IMPROVE THEIR STRENGTH AND MOBILITY

DOWN

2. THE TEAM LEADER ON THE ICE IF THE CAPTAIN IS OFF THE ICE
3. THEY PROTECT THE GOAL
6. THEY PLAY LEFT OF THE CENTER
8. THEY MONITOR THE TIME
10. THEY PROTECT THE DEFENSIVE ZONE

Collins (#33), center for the Tigers, attempts
a **one-on-one** with only Robinson (#34), defenseman
for the Mustangs, between him and the goal.

GOAL SCORED

Bure (#4), center for the Tigers, **dekes** the
Mustangs' goalie and scores a goal.

GOAL SCORED

SPOT THE DIFFERENCES
Can you spot the **ten** differences between
this drawing and the one on page 88?

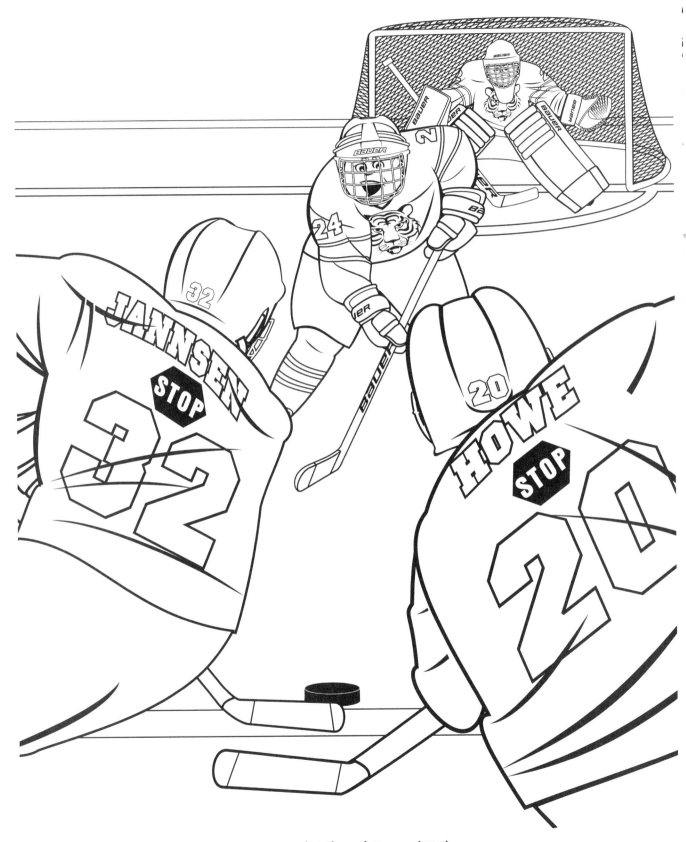

Jannsen (#32) and Howe (#20),
left wing and center for the Mustangs,
make an **odd-man rush** on the Tigers' net.

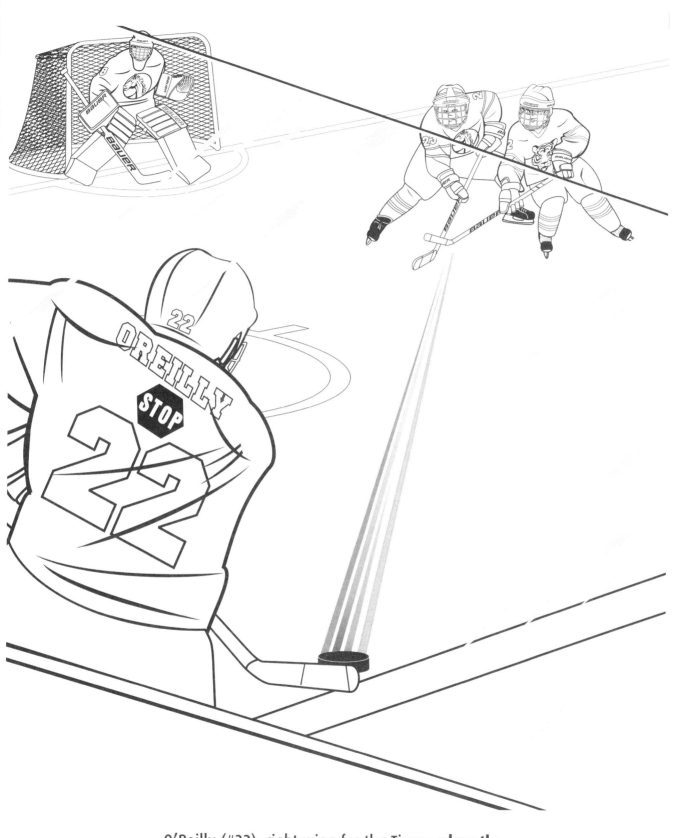

O'Reilly (#22), right wing for the Tigers, **plays the point** and gets set to receive the puck from defenseman Eriksson (#12).

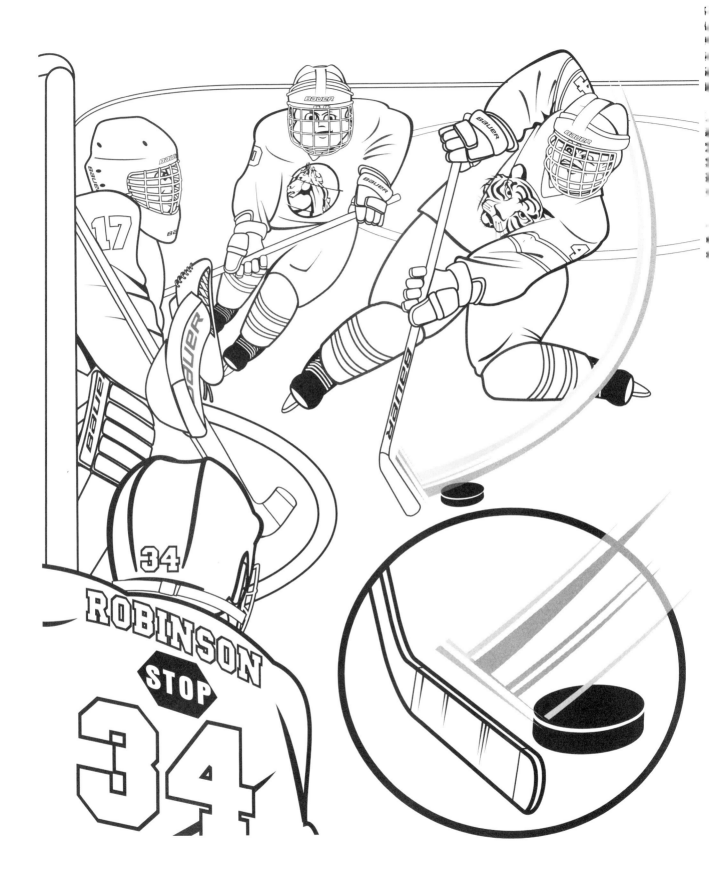

 92

Bure (#4), center for the Tigers, missed a great opportunity
to score a goal when he **fanned** on the shot.

WORD SCRAMBLE #2
D-H

UNSCRAMBLE THE LETTERS AND USE THE CLUE
TO FIND THE CORRECT HOCKEY TERM.

Scramble	Clue	
OWINGLBE	USE PART OF THE ARM	_____
ECAF-FOF	STARTS PLAY	_____
ATLF ASSP	STAYS ON ICE	_____
PILF SPSA	UP IN THE AIR	_____
RADFWRO	OUT FRONT	_____
OALG	GET A POINT	_____
NETDERLAOG	PROTECTS NET	_____
ALOGTSOP	HOLDS CROSSBAR	_____
DNAH SSPA	WITH A BODY PART	_____
TAH RIKCT	GET THREE GOALS	_____
LMEHET	PROTECTS HEAD	_____
EERERFE	CONTROLS GAME	_____
HHGI GNICITSK	KEEP IT DOWN	_____
LDINGOH	DON'T LET GO	_____
OKGOHIN	ILLEGAL STICK USE	_____

GO TIGERS GO

ICE CLEANING MAZE

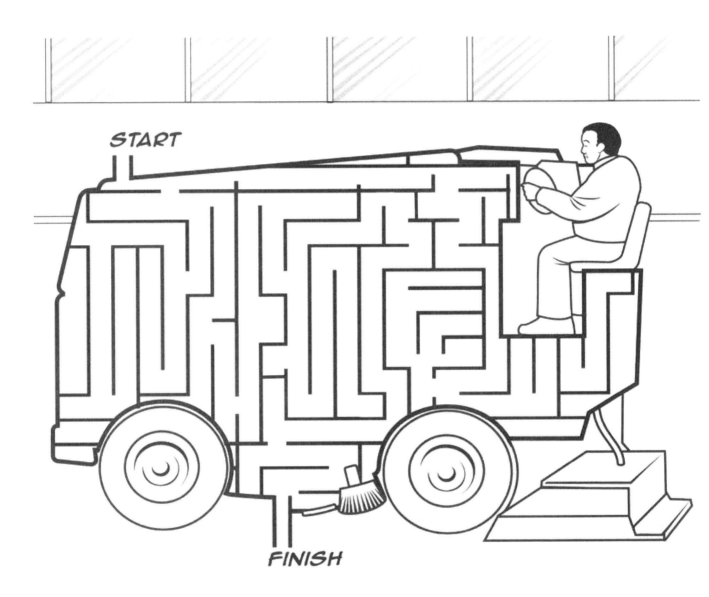

START

FINISH

Find your way through the ice-resurfacing machine.

Walker (#26), defenseman for the Mustangs, shows
commitment by **blocking** the shot on goal.

CANADA

CONNECT THE DOTS
The ice is cleaned between the periods to ensure
a clean, smooth ice surface for the game.

The **team captains** conference with the referee
to get an explanation on a call.

 98

The **referee** and **linesmen** control the game.
Players **MUST** respect the calls that officials make.

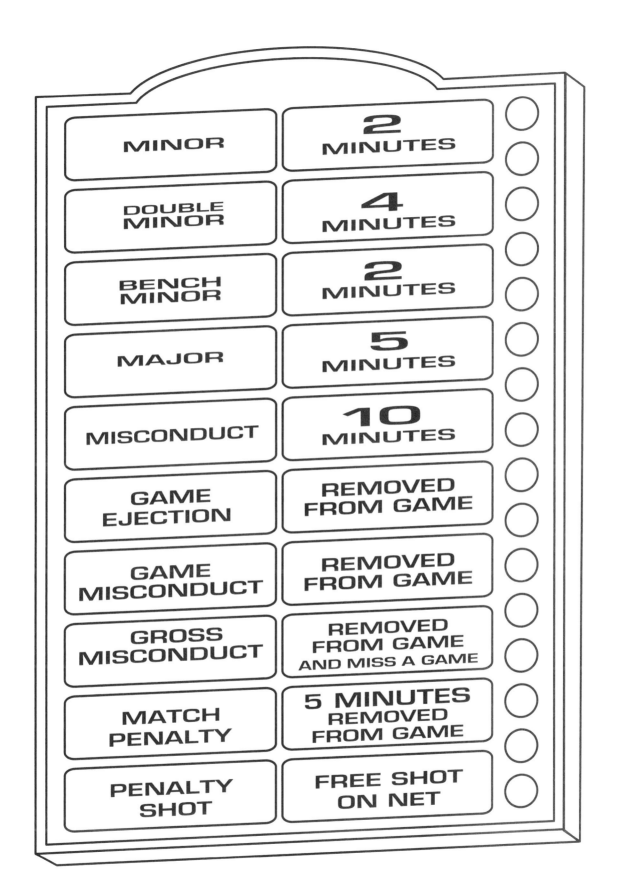

MINOR	**2** MINUTES
DOUBLE MINOR	**4** MINUTES
BENCH MINOR	**2** MINUTES
MAJOR	**5** MINUTES
MISCONDUCT	**10** MINUTES
GAME EJECTION	REMOVED FROM GAME
GAME MISCONDUCT	REMOVED FROM GAME
GROSS MISCONDUCT	REMOVED FROM GAME AND MISS A GAME
MATCH PENALTY	**5 MINUTES** REMOVED FROM GAME
PENALTY SHOT	FREE SHOT ON NET

The severity of the infraction determines
the length of the penalty.

TRIPPING

 100

Lui (#5), defenseman for the Tigers, is given a
two-minute penalty for **tripping**.

PENALTY SHOT

Lopez (#31), center for the Mustangs,
takes a **penalty shot** because a Tigers player
tripped him on a breakaway.

MATCH THE DESCRIPTION TO THE CORRECT HOCKEY TERM

_____ FORECHECK   _____ GOALTENDER   _____ FOREHAND SHOT
_____ GOAL LINE   _____ FLAT PASS   _____ FREEZE THE PUCK
_____ FORWARDS   _____ FLIPSHOT   _____ GOAL CREASE
_____ FULL STRENGTH   _____ GOAL   _____ GAME MISCONDUCT

DESCRIPTION

1. When a player passes the puck to a teammate along the surface of the ice.

2. When a player flips the puck up off the ice as they take a shot on the goal.

3. To check an opposing player in their defensive zone while trying to regain control of the puck.

4. When a right-handed player takes the shot from their right side or a left-handed player takes the shot from their left side.

5. The three players that make up the attacking line of a team; the center, right wing, and left wing.

6. When a player holds the puck against the boards with their skate or stick in order to stop the play and gain a face-off.

7. When a team has all six players on the ice.

8. A penalty that suspends a player for the remainder of the game but allows the team to send in a substitute player.

9. When a team gets a point by shooting the puck into the net.

10. The player whose job it is to keep the puck out of the net.

11. The semicircle area in the front of the net where the goalie can play without being obstructed by opposing players.

12. The red line between the goalposts that the puck must cross in order to count as a goal.

GAME 5

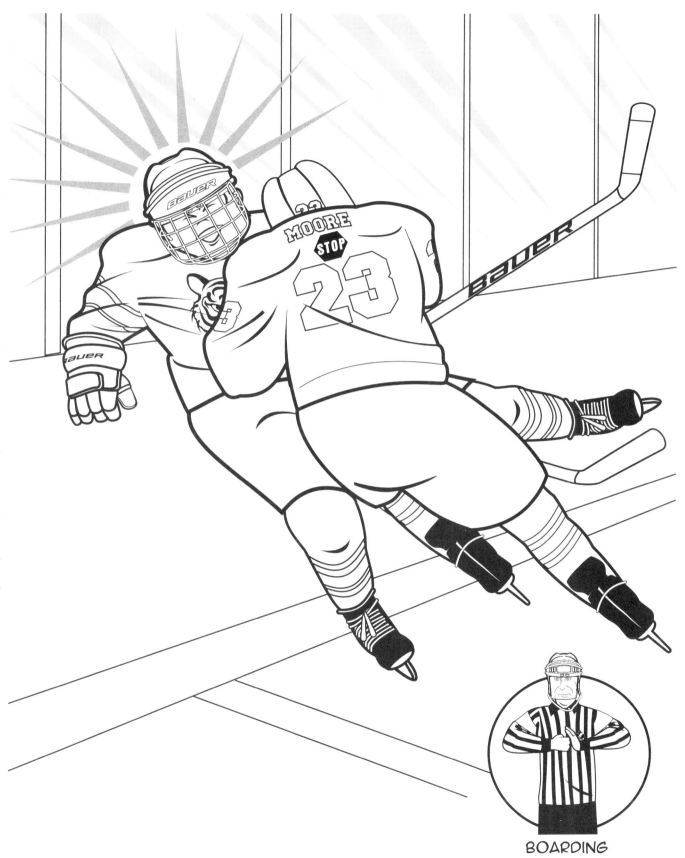

BOARDING

Moore (#23), defenseman for the Mustangs, is given a
penalty for **boarding**.

HOLDING

 104

Bianchi (#14), defenseman for the Mustangs, is given a
two-minute penalty for **holding**.

PLAYS AND SHOTS WORD SEARCH

```
A C E N T E R I N G
Y D N A H E R O F O
A H S S A V E N A A
W A H K N S T O C L
A T O A D O I R E P
K T O T P U E A O G
A R T I A T M U F A
E I T N S W T P F G
R C R G S I H U S A
B K E N O N O E N O
S F H A S S I S T D
```

CENTERING   WIN   BREAKAWAY

CENTERING	WIN	BREAKAWAY
HAND PASS	ASSIST	DUMP
FACE-OFF	SHOOT	HAT TRICK
ONE-ON-ONE	TIE	GOAL
FOREHAND	SAVE	SKATING

Find all the words which relate to plays
and shots during the game.

INTERFERENCE

Vanderby (#19), right wing for the Tigers,
is given a two-minute penalty
for **goalie interference**.

106

HOCKEY TERMS CROSSWORD

ACROSS

3. WHEN THE PUCK BOUNCES OFF A GOALIE'S BLOCKER OR PAD

6. WHEN MULTIPLE PLAYERS FIGHT FOR CONTROL OF THE PUCK

8. THE PASS TO A TEAMMATE THAT SCORES A GOAL

9. TO PASS THE PUCK SLIGHTLY AHEAD OF THE INTENDED TARGET

11. IT IS TAKEN AT THE START OF EACH PERIOD

12. TO GET BY AN OPPOSING PLAYER AND GO IN ALONE ON THE GOAL

13. TO GET THREE GOALS IN A SINGLE GAME.

15. IF THE PUCK CROSSES THE RED LINE BUT DOES NOT GO IN THE GOAL AND IS TOUCHED BY AN OPPOSING PLAYER FIRST

DOWN

1. WHEN BOTH SKATES OF AN OPPOSING PLAYER CROSS THE BLUE LINE AHEAD OF THE PUCK

2. WHEN A TEAM LOSES CONTROL OF THE PUCK TO THE OPPOSING TEAM

4. AN ADDITIONAL PERIOD OF PLAY TO DETERMINE A WINNER

5. WHEN A PLAYER DELIBERATELY FALLS TO DRAW A PENALTY

7. TO STOP THE PUCK FROM ENTERING THE GOAL

10. WHEN THE PUCK BOUNCES OFF THE GOALPOST OR A SKATE

14. WHEN CONTACT IS MADE WITH AN OPPOSING PLAYER TO GAIN AN ADVANTAGE

TRIPPING

Coach Murphy from the Tigers will have to
select another player to take the two-minute penalty
for **tripping** given to goalie DeVries (#1).

CHECKING
FROM BEHIND

Schroder (#7), right wing for the Mustangs, is
given a penalty for **checking from behind**.
This is a very dangerous check!

HOOKING

Eriksson (#12), defenseman for the Tigers,
is given a two-minute penalty for **hooking**.

_____ LINESMAN _____ LEAD PASS _____ HOOKING

_____ HASH MARKS _____ INTERFERENCE _____ HAT TRICK

_____ KNEEING _____ HOLDING _____ LINE CHANGE

_____ HIGH-STICKING _____ ICING _____ HIP CHECK

DESCRIPTION

1. When a player scores three goals in a single game.

2. The two-foot lines that extend from the face-off circles that help the wingers determine their position during the face-off.

3. When a player holds their stick above an opposing player's shoulders and hits or threatens the opposing player.

4. A legal check using your hip.

5. When a player grabs an opposing player to impede their progress.

6. When a player tries to slow the progress of an opposing player using the part of their stick where the blade is attached to the shaft.

7. When the team in possession of the puck shoots it from behind the center red line across the opposing team's goal line resulting in a face-off in the offending team's defensive zone.

8. When a player tries to impede the motion of a player not in possession of the puck.

9. When a player uses their knee to hit an opposing player in the leg, thigh, or lower body.

10. When a player passes the puck slightly ahead of a teammate.

11. The two officials on the ice other than the referee.

12. When an entire forward or defensive line is changed at the same time.

GAME 6

Bower (#27), defenseman for the Mustangs,
is given a two-minute penalty
for **elbowing**.

ELBOWING

Vanderby (#19), right wing for the Tigers,
is given a five-minute penalty and a
game misconduct for **kneeing**.

KNEEING

113

HIGH-STICKING

 114

Moretti (#9), left wing for the Tigers, is given
a penalty for **high-sticking**.

Move the puck from start to finish
in order to score a goal!

WORD SCRAMBLE #3
H-R

UNSCRAMBLE THE LETTERS AND USE THE CLUE TO FIND THE CORRECT HOCKEY TERM.

GNICI	CROSS TOO MANY LINES	_____
RENCEFIENETR	GET IN THE WAY	_____
NAMSENIL	HELPS THE REFEREE	_____
UTRALEN ENOZ	BETWEEN THE BLUE LINES	_____
DESIFFO	NOT ONSIDE	_____
ENO-NO-NEO	MAN-TO-MAN	_____
LTYANEP	INFRACTION	_____
IORDPE	ONE OF THREE	_____
INTOP	SCORE A GOAL	_____
OKEP ECKHC	CHECK WITH STICK	_____
SSSPOSEINO	HAVE CONTROL	_____
OWERP YALP	EXTRA MAN	_____
DER LEIN	CENTER OF RINK	_____
EREEFRE	CONTROLS THE GAME	_____
GHINGROU	ALMOST FIGHTING	_____

BENCH MINOR

The Tigers receive a **bench minor**;
they had too many players on the ice.

MATCH THE DESCRIPTION TO THE CORRECT HOCKEY TERM

_____ POKE CHECK   _____ PENALTY SHOT   _____ PENALTY BOX

_____ ONE-ON-ONE   _____ MAJOR PENALTY   _____ POINT

_____ OVERTIME   _____ OUT-OF-PLAY   _____ MINOR PENALTY

_____ NEUTRAL ZONE   _____ OFFSIDE   _____ PENALTY KILLER

DESCRIPTION

1. A more serious penalty for which the offending player will stay off the ice for five minutes whether a goal is scored or not. In minor hockey, the player will be removed for the remainder of the game.

2. A less serious penalty for which the offending player will be off the ice for two minutes or until a goal is scored.

3. The area between the blue lines.

4. When both skates of an attacking player cross the opposing team's blue line before the puck is passed or carried into the attacking zone.

5. When an attacking player has the puck and there is only one opposing player between them and the goalie.

6. When the puck goes over the boards, over the glass, or into one of the team's benches.

7. An additional period of play used to break a tie.

8. Where players go to serve the time given for their penalty.

9. A player that is good at backchecking and gaining control of a loose puck when their team is shorthanded.

10. A free shot on the goalie awarded to a player who was interfered with that prevented them from a clear scoring opportunity.

11. A quick thrust to the puck or opposing player's stick to knock the puck away from them.

12. The left and right positions of the ice surface that the defensemen for the attacking team play, just inside the blue line of the attacking zone.

GAME 7

INTERFERENCE

Bianchi (#14), defenseman for the Mustangs, is given
a two-minute penalty for **interference**.

SLASHING

 O'Sullivan (#28), defenseman for the Tigers, is given
a two-minute penalty for **slashing**.

DELAYING
THE GAME

Smith (#30), center for the Tigers, is given
a two-minute penalty; he deliberately **delayed the
game** by shooting the puck over the glass.

121

INTERFERENCE
WITH GOALTENDER

Howe (#20), center for the Mustangs, is given
a two-minute penalty for interference;
he is **in the Tiger goal crease**.

INTERFERENCE
WITH GOALTENDER

SPOT THE DIFFERENCES
Can you spot the **ten** differences between
this drawing and the one on page 122?

MATCH THE DESCRIPTION TO THE CORRECT HOCKEY TERM

_____ SAVE   _____ POWER PLAY   _____ REFEREE'S CREASE

_____ ROUGHING   _____ RED LINE   _____ REBOUND

_____ SHIFT   _____ SCREEN SHOT   _____ SCRAMBLE

_____ SHADOW   _____ REFEREE   _____ PULL THE GOALIE

DESCRIPTION

1. When a team has more players on the ice due to a penalty or penalties by the opposing team.

2. When the goalie comes off the ice and is replaced by a sixth skater.

3. When a puck bounces off the goalie's body or equipment.

4. The line that divides the ice surface in half.

5. The head, on-ice official in a hockey game.

6. The ten-foot (3.05m) semicircle marked in red in front of the timekeeper's bench.

7. When two opposing players push and shove each other.

8. When a goalie stops the puck from entering the goal.

9. When several players from both teams fight for possession of the puck.

10. A shot on the goal that the goalie cannot see due to the other players blocking his view.

11. When one player closely follows an opposing player to prevent them from making a play.

12. The time that a player is on the ice playing and not on the bench.

DELAYED PENALTY

Schroder (#7), right wing for the Mustangs, holds
O'Reilly (#22), right wing for the Tigers. Let's see if
Smith (#30), center for the Tigers, scores a goal.

WASHOUT

A goal scored by Lopez (#31), center for the Mustangs, is disallowed due to a penalty called on one of his teammates.

ROUGHING

Binda (#31), left wing for the Tigers, and
Miller (#25), right wing for the Mustangs, are each
given a two-minute penalty for **roughing**.

127

 128

MISCONDUCT

Any major penalty in minor or female hockey
is an automatic **game misconduct**.

PENALTY WORD SEARCH

```
C G N I P P I R T O I E A
C N R B B U N I U S A C G
C I M S E L B O W I N G N
O K I E P S L A S H I N G
E C N E R E F R E T N I N
N E R N B O A R D I N G I
R H O K H H S R E N A R K
T C U D N O C S I M N A O
M Y G B S E L N G N R H O
I D H D R I E D E Y G C H
N O I I E N D I I B O S R
O B N O N C D R N N G A K
R T G I L O R G I G G N G
```

BENCH	BOARDING	ELBOWING
TRIPPING	ROUGHING	SLASHING
HOOKING	MISCONDUCT	KNEEING
HOLDING	CHARGING	BODYCHECKING
SPEARING	INTERFERENCE	MINOR

 129

Find all the words which relate to penalties.

HOLDING AN
OPPOSING
PLAYER'S STICK

Howe (#20), center for the Mustangs, is given
a two-minute penalty for **holding the stick**
of Lui (#5), defenseman for the Tigers.

_____ STICKHANDLE   _____ SPEARING   _____ TOP-SHELF GOAL

_____ SHOOTOUT   _____ SWEEP CHECK   _____ SUDDEN DEATH OVERTIME

_____ SLAPSHOT   _____ SLASHING   _____ SHORTHANDED GOAL

                  _____ SLOT   _____ SPLIT THE DEFENSE

DESCRIPTION

1. A competition used in a tied game to determine which team wins.

2. A goal scored by a team that is killing a penalty.

3. A shot where the player raises his stick up to shoulder-level or higher on the backswing before swinging it forward and connecting with the puck.

4. When a player swings the blade of his stick at an opposing player.

5. The thirty-foot (9.14m) area in front of the net, the prime area for scoring goals.

6. When a player jabs or attempts to jab the point of the blade of their stick into an opposing player.

7. When a player in possession of the puck skates between the two defensemen from the opposing team.

8. The term for handling the puck with the hockey stick.

9. An extra period that ends as soon as one of the two competing teams scores a goal.

10. A check made by a player with one hand on their stick and one knee almost touching the ice while making a sweeping motion with their stick to take the puck from an opposing player.

11. When a player shoots the puck into the top corner of the net above the goalie's shoulder.

GAME 9

HOCKEY PENALTIES CROSSWORD

ACROSS
3. WHEN A PLAYER SWINGS THEIR STICK AT AN OPPOSING PLAYER WITH ONE OR BOTH HANDS
4. WHEN A PLAYER BECOMES OVERLY AGGRESSIVE WITH AN OPPOSING PLAYER
6. WHEN A PLAYER TAKES TWO OR MORE STRIDES PRIOR TO CONTACT WITH AN OPPOSING PLAYER
10. WHEN A TEAM HAS LESS PLAYERS ON THE ICE THAN THE OPPOSING TEAM
11. WHEN A PLAYER POKES AN OPPOSING PLAYER WITH THE TOE OF THEIR STICK
12. A PENALTY GIVEN FOR HAVING TOO MANY PLAYERS ON THE ICE
13. WHEN A PLAYER IMPEDES THE PROGRESS OF AN OPPOSING PLAYER WITH THE HOOK OF THEIR STICK
14. WHEN A PLAYER HANGS ONTO AN OPPOSING PLAYER AND SLOWS THEIR PROGRESS
15. WHEN A PLAYER USES THE SHAFT OF THEIR STICK HELD BETWEEN TWO HANDS TO CHECK AN OPPOSING PLAYER WITH THEIR STICK

DOWN
1. A RESULT IF A RULE OF HOCKEY IS BROKEN
2. WHEN A PLAYER STRIKES AN OPPOSING PLAYER WITH THEIR ELBOW
5. WHERE A PLAYER GOES IF GIVEN A PENALTY (2 WORDS)
7. WHEN A PLAYER IMPEDES THE PROGRESS OF AN OPPOSING PLAYER NOT IN POSSESSION OF THE PUCK
8. WHEN A PLAYER HOLDS THEIR STICK ABOVE THE NORMAL HEIGHT OF AN OPPOSING PLAYER'S SHOULDER
9. WHEN A PLAYER VIOLENTLY CHECKS AN OPPOSING PLAYER AGAINST THE BOARDS

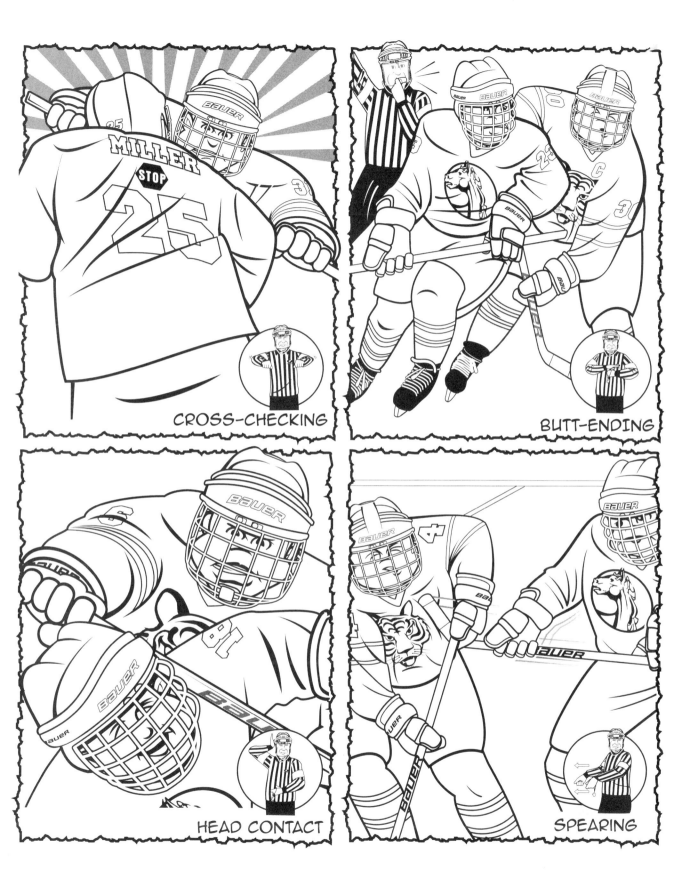

CROSS-CHECKING

BUTT-ENDING

HEAD CONTACT

SPEARING

There is no room in hockey for unsportsmanlike conduct
or actions that can cause serious injury to players.

Garcia (#21), left wing for the Tigers, receives a two-minute penalty for having an **illegal hockey stick**.

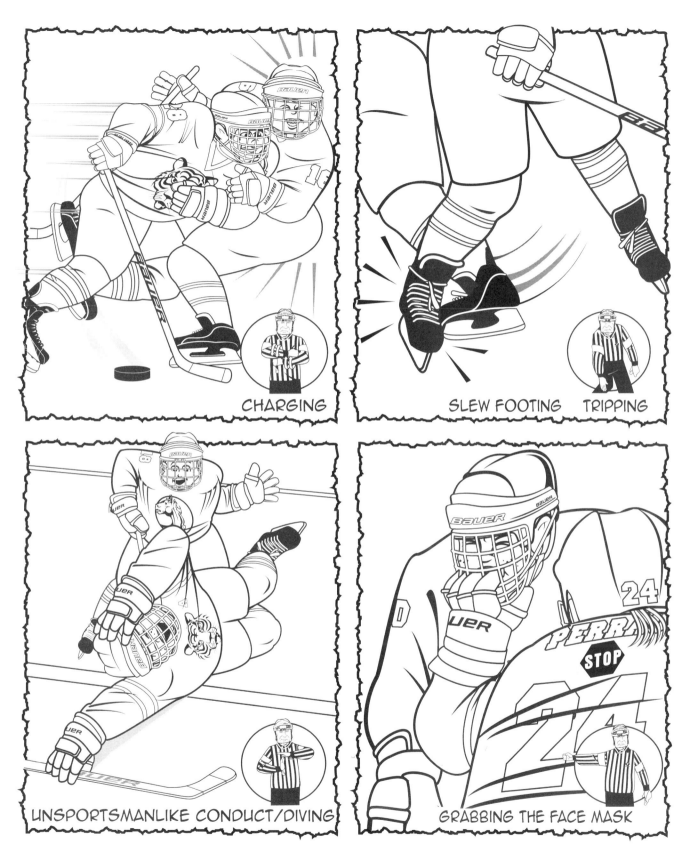

There is no room in hockey for unsportsmanlike conduct
or actions that can cause serious injury to players.

OFFICIAL'S SIGNAL GAME

MATCH THE OFFICIAL'S SIGNAL TO THE CORRECT ACTION OR PENALTY

_____BOARDING   _____ELBOWING   _____CHECKING FROM BEHIND
_____CHARGING   _____HIGH-STICKING _____WASHOUT
_____HAND PASS   _____HOOKING   _____HEAD CONTACT
                  _____SPEARING   _____DELAYED OFFSIDE

1

2

3

4

5

6

7

8

9

10

11

GAME 1

OFFICIAL'S SIGNAL GAME

MATCH THE OFFICIAL'S SIGNAL TO THE CORRECT ACTION OR PENALTY

_____ DELAY OF GAME
_____ GOAL SCORED
_____ GRABBING FACE MASK
_____ HOLDING OPPONENT'S STICK

_____ HOOKING
_____ SPEARING
_____ HOLDING

_____ OFFSIDE
_____ INTERFERENCE
_____ INTERFERENCE WITH GOALTENDER

1

2

3

4

5

6

7

8

9

10

GAME 2

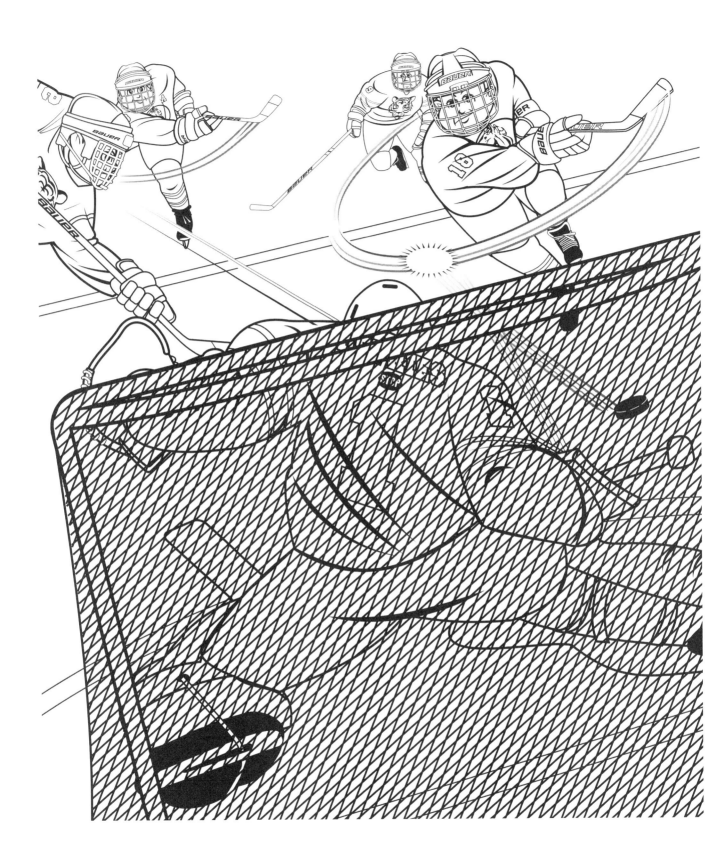

Havel (#18), left wing for the Mustangs, shoots the
goalie's **rebound** back towards the net.
Watch out for rebounds!

Singh (#23), defenseman for the Tigers, **shadows** Owens (#29), left wing for the Mustangs. He'll be right there if Owens is passed the puck.

Becker (#15) and Garcia (#21), wingers for the
Tigers, **split the defense** and **clear the slot**
for Bure (#4), center for the Tigers.

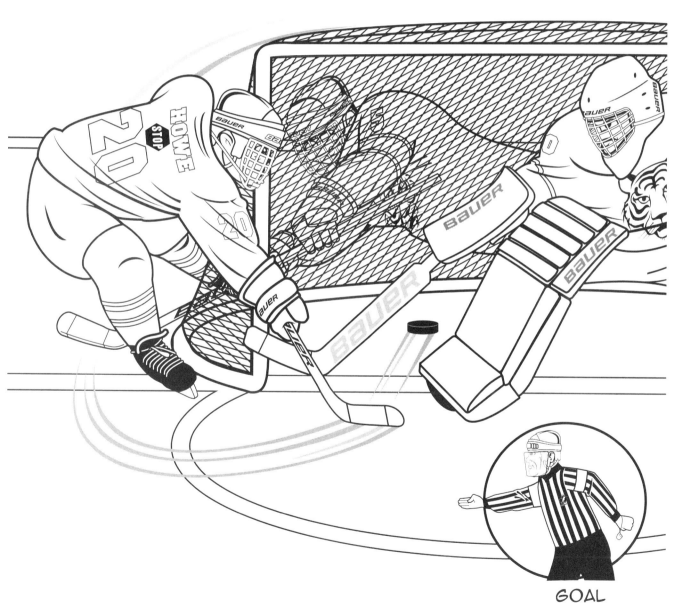

GOAL

Howe (#20), center for the Mustangs, scores
a **wraparound goal**.

Bower (#27), defenseman for the Mustangs, gets the **deflection** off the goalpost. The Mustangs were lucky!

WORD SCRAMBLE #4
S-Z

UNSCRAMBLE THE LETTERS AND USE THE CLUE TO FIND THE CORRECT HOCKEY TERM.

VEAS	STOP THE PUCK	_____
TOHOSTUO	DETERMINE A WINNER	_____
DNAHTROHDES	MISSING A PLAYER	_____
TEAKS	HAS A BLADE	_____
PASLOTHS	A HARD SHOT	_____
SHINGLAS	ILLEGAL STICK USE	_____
YANLSTE UPC	GRAND PRIZE	_____
KCITS	IMPORTANT TOOL	_____
EWEPS KCEHC	LOW CHECK	_____
TEMI-UTO	TAKE A BREAK	_____
RIPIPNTG	CAUSE TO FALL	_____
VOERNRUT	LOSE THE PUCK	_____
ERGINW	PLAYS THE SIDE	_____
ISRTW HOTS	TYPE OF SHOT	_____

 144

Collins (#33), center for the Tigers, scores
a **top-shelf goal.**

GOAL

Tigers' defenseman Singh (#23) and right winger
Becker (#15) receive **assists** for the goal scored by Bure (#4).
It's all about teamwork!

Havel (#18), left wing for the Mustangs, is
in the penalty box. This gives the Tigers
a **man advantage**.

O'Connor (#10), center for the Mustangs, scores a
goal while **shorthanded**.

GOAL

 150

Sanders (#6), defenseman for the Tigers, is about to take a
screened shot onto the Mustangs' goal.

SPOT THE DIFFERENCES
Can you spot the **ten** differences between
this drawing and the one on page 150?

151

O'Connor (#10), center for the Mustangs, enters
the game when the goalie, Taylor (#8), is
pulled by Coach Murphy.

Smith (#30), center for the Tigers, scores an
empty-net goal.

153

Lopez (#3), center for the Mustangs, skates
towards the Tigers' goal in the **shootout**
to break the tie.

154

MATCH THE DESCRIPTION TO THE CORRECT HOCKEY TERM

_____ WASHOUT　　_____ TWO-ON-TWO　　_____ WINGS

_____ ZAMBONI™　　_____ TRAILER　　_____ WRAPAROUND

_____ TURNOVER　　_____ WRIST SHOT　　_____ TRAP

_____ TRIPPING　　_____ ZONES

DESCRIPTION

1. The player skating behind a teammate in order to be in position to take a drop pass.

2. A defensive formation designed to minimize the opposing team's ability to score.

3. When a player uses their stick or their body around the feet or legs of an opposing player to cause them to lose their balance.

4. When one team loses control of the puck to the opposing team.

5. When two attacking players must get by one of the opposing team's defensemen.

6. When a goal is ruled invalid by the referee or when the linesman waves off a penalty.

7. The two players that are on each side of the center.

8. When an attacking player skates behind the net and scores by wrapping the puck around the post.

9. A shot made by flicking the wrist and forearm.

10. A brand of ice-cleaning machine used to clean the ice surface before a game and between periods.

11. The attacking, neutral, and defending areas between the two blue lines.

GAME 10

Always show **good sportsmanship**
at the end of a game.

THE TIGERS

THE MUSTANGS

A positive team effort on the part of the players,
coaches, parents, and officials ensures a
rewarding hockey experience.

MATCH GAME ANSWERS
#1–#5

MATCH GAME 1 PAGE 39

_9_ BREAKAWAY   _8_ BLOCKED SHOT   _4_ BLIND PASS
_6_ BOARDS   _1_ ASSIST   _11_ BENCH MINOR
_12_ BACKHAND   _7_ BODYCHECK   _5_ BLUE LINE
_3_ BACKCHECK   _10_ BLOCKER   _2_ ATTACKING ZONE

MATCH GAME 2 PAGE 51

_10_ CREASE   _5_ CENTER ICE   _12_ CLEARING THE PUCK
_4_ CENTER   _3_ CATCHER   _8_ FACE-OFF CIRCLE
_11_ CHECK   _7_ CENTERING   _9_ CHANGE ON THE FLY
_2_ BOX   _6_ CENTER LINE   _1_ BREAKAWAY PASS

MATCH GAME 3 PAGE 65

_6_ CROSSBAR   _11_ COVER   _3_ DEFENSIVE ZONE
_5_ DEKE THE GOALIE   _8_ DELAY OF GAME   _10_ CLEARING THE ZONE
_9_ CROSS CHECK   _12_ DEFENSIVE LINE   _1_ DEAD PUCK
_2_ DEFENSEMEN   _4_ DEFLECTION   _7_ DELAYED CALL

MATCH GAME 4 PAGE 79

_10_ FACE-OFF   _6_ ELBOWING   _1_ DELAYED OFFSIDE
_4_ DROP PASS   _5_ DUMP AND CHASE   _9_ EXTRA ATTACKER
_8_ EVEN STRENGTH   _3_ DOUBLE MINOR   _7_ EMPTY-NET GOAL
_2_ HAND PASS   _11_ FACE-OFF CIRCLES AND DOTS

MATCH GAME 5 PAGE 102

_3_ FORECHECK   _10_ GOALTENDER   _4_ FOREHAND SHOT
_12_ GOAL LINE   _1_ FLAT PASS   _6_ FREEZE THE PUCK
_5_ FORWARDS   _2_ FLIP SHOT   _11_ GOAL CREASE
_7_ FULL STRENGTH   _9_ GOAL   _8_ GAME MISCONDUCT

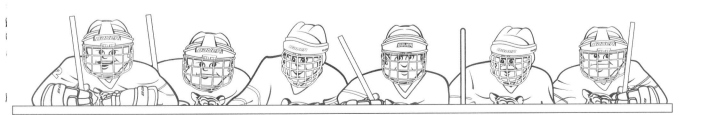

MATCH GAME ANSWERS
#6-#10

MATCH GAME 6 PAGE 111

_11_ LINESMAN
_2_ HASH MARKS
_9_ KNEEING
_3_ HIGH-STICKING

_6_ HOOKING
_1_ HAT TRICK
_12_ LINE CHANGE
_4_ HIP CHECK

_10_ LEAD PASS
_8_ INTERFERENCE
_5_ HOLDING
_7_ ICING

MATCH GAME 7 PAGE 118

_11_ POKE CHECK
_5_ ONE-ON-ONE
_7_ OVERTIME
_3_ NEUTRAL ZONE

_10_ PENALTY SHOT
_1_ MAJOR PENALTY
_6_ OUT-OF-PLAY
_4_ OFFSIDE

_8_ PENALTY BOX
_12_ POINT
_2_ MINOR PENALTY
_9_ PENALTY KILLER

MATCH GAME 8 PAGE 124

_8_ SAVE
_7_ ROUGHING
_12_ SHIFT
_11_ SHADOW

_1_ POWER PLAY
_4_ RED LINE
_10_ SCREEN SHOT
_5_ REFEREE

_6_ REFEREE'S CREASE
_3_ REBOUND
_9_ SCRAMBLE
_2_ PULL THE GOALIE

MATCH GAME 9 PAGE 131

_8_ STICKHANDLE
_1_ SHOOTOUT
_3_ SLAPSHOT

_6_ SPEARING
_10_ SWEEP CHECK
_4_ SLASHING
_5_ SLOT

_12_ TOP-SHELF GOAL
_9_ SUDDEN DEATH OVERTIME
_2_ SHORTHANDED GOAL
_7_ SPLIT THE DEFENSE

MATCH GAME 10 PAGE 155

_6_ WASHOUT
_10_ ZAMBONI™
_4_ TURNOVER
_3_ TRIPPING

_5_ TWO-ON-ONE
_1_ TRAILER
_9_ WRIST SHOT
_11_ ZONES

_7_ WINGS
_8_ WRAPAROUND
_2_ TRAP

SPOT THE DIFFERENCES ANSWERS

SPOT THE DIFFERENCES PAGE 10

SPOT THE DIFFERENCES PAGE 11

FIND TEN HOCKEY STICKS PAGES 16 AND 17

SPOT THE DIFFERENCE GAME ANSWERS

SPOT THE DIFFERENCES PAGE 55

SPOT THE DIFFERENCES PAGE 89

SPOT THE DIFFERENCES PAGE 123

SPOT THE DIFFERENCES PAGE 151

MAZE
ANSWERS

SKATE MAZE: PAGE 38

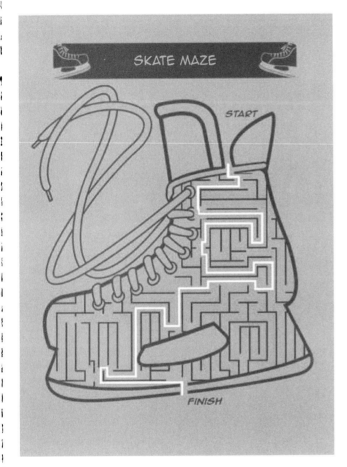

GOALIE MAZE: PAGE 72

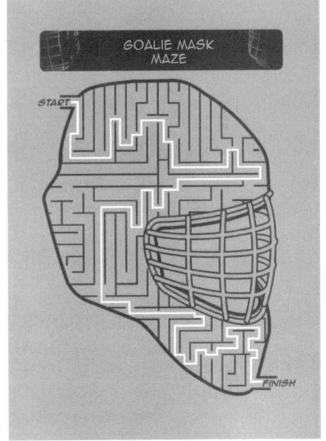

MAZE ANSWERS

ICE CLEANING MAZE: PAGE 94

HOCKEY RINK MAZE: PAGE 120

WORD SEARCH ANSWERS

EQUIPMENT PAGE 30

```
H U K C U P A T E N
O G S B L A D E S E
C A A O L A O T T G
K M M A P O T A E K
E E E R A C S M A
Y C C D A P T K L U
B L A N P T C A E H
A O F T S T P A T R
G C G L O V E E A C
A K N I R N Q S R A
```

PEOPLE PAGE 63

```
E N D R A W R O F T
T N I R E Y A L P A R
N A T L E F T W I N G
A T I I O T E A M S N
S P N F S E N E Z I
S I C E A T T C S H W
I S C O A C H E T
S E M R O S T E R H
S R E N I A R T T G
A I N G O A L I E I
H O M E T E A M A R
```

PLAYS & SHOTS PAGE 105

```
A C E N T E R I N G
Y D N A H E R O F O
A H S S A V E N O A
W A H K N S T O C L
A T O A D O I R E P
K R T T P U E A O G
A I T I A T M U F A
E C N S W T P F F
R K E N O N O E N O
B S F H A S S I S T D
```

PENALTIES PAGE 129

```
C G N I P P I R T O I E A
C N R B B U N I U S A C G
C I M S E L B O W I N G N
O K I E P S L A S H I N G
E C N E R E F R E T N I N
N E R N B O A R D I N G I
R H O K H H S R E N A R K
T C U D N O C S I M N A O
M Y G B S E L N G N R H O
I D H D R I E D E Y G C H
N O I I E N D I I B O S R
O B N O N C D R N N G A K
R T G I L O R G I G G N G
```

167

OFFICIAL'S SIGNAL GAME ANSWERS

GAME 1

PAGE 136

5 BOARDING
8 CHARGING
7 HAND PASS

1 ELBOWING
11 HIGH-STICKING
3 HOOKING
10 SPEARING

9 CHECKING FROM BEHIND
6 WASHOUT
2 CHECKING TO THE HEAD
4 DELAYED OFFSIDE

GAME 2

PAGE 137

1 DELAY OF GAME
6 GOAL SCORED
7 GRABBING FACE MASK
10 HOLDING OPPONENT'S STICK

9 HOOKING
2 SPEARING
5 HOLDING

4 OFFSIDE
3 INTERFERENCE
8 INTERFERENCE WITH GOALTENDER

WORD SCRAMBLE ANSWERS

PAGE 73 LETTERS A-D

ASSIST
BLOCKER
BACKHAND
BREAKAWAY
CATCHER
CAPTAIN
CENTER
CHARGING
CHECK
COACH
CREASE
CROSSBAR
DEFENSEMEN
DIVE
DROP PASS

PAGE 93 LETTERS D-H

ELBOWING
FACE-OFF
FLAT PASS
FLIP PASS
FORWARD
GOAL
GOALTENDER
GOALPOST
HAND PASS
HAT TRICK
HELMET
REFEREE
HIGH-STICKING
HOLDING
HOOKING

PAGE 116 LETTERS H-R

ICING
INTERFERENCE
LINESMAN
NEUTRAL ZONE
OFFSIDE
ONE-ON-ONE
PENALTY
PERIOD
POINT
POKE CHECK
POSSESSION
POWER PLAY
RED LINE
REFEREE
ROUGHING

PAGE 143 LETTERS S-Z

SAVE
SHOOTOUT
SHORTHANDED
SKATE
SLAPSHOT
SLASHING
STANLEY CUP
STICK
SWEEP CHECK
TIME OUT
TRIPPING
TURNOVER
WINGER
WRIST SHOT

CROSSWORD SOLUTIONS

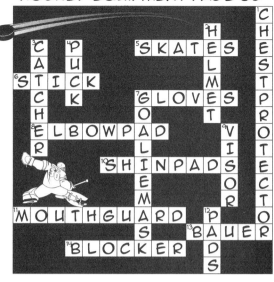

HOCKEY EQUIPMENT PAGE 56

```
                          ²H        ¹C
   ³C   ⁴P              ⁵S K A T E S  H E S T
   A    U                          L  P
  ⁶S T I C K            ⁷G L O V E S M  R
   T    C                          E  O  O
   C    K              G          T  V  T
  ⁸E L B O W P A D      O      ⁹V I S O R
   H                    A         I  O  E
          ¹⁰S H I N P A D S       V  R  C
   R                   L          O      T
  ¹¹M O U T H G U A R D I   ¹²P   R      O
                       E    A            R
                       M   ¹³B A U E R
  ¹⁴B L O C K E R           D
                            S
```

HOCKEY ARENA TERMS PAGE 58

```
                ²B O ¹A R D S
   ³P    ⁵I      T              ⁴N
   E    ⁵I C    T          ⁶F   E
  ⁷F A C E O F F C I R C L E A   U
   N    L        C          C   T
   A    T       ⁸R          E   R
   L   ⁹B L U E L I N E     O   A
   T    Y        F      ¹⁰P F   L
  ¹¹G O A L L I N E E    L  F   Z
   Y    X        R      A   S   O
          ¹²D E F E N S I V E Z O N E
                 E      E   P   E
                 C      R   O
  ¹³H A S H M A R K S   S   T
                 E      B
  ¹⁴G O A L C R E A S E N
                 S      C
            ¹⁵N E T     H
```

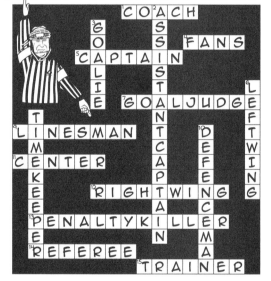

HOCKEY PERSONNEL PAGE 86

```
                 ¹C O ²C A C H
               ³G    S
               O    S      ⁴F A N S
              ⁵C A P T A I N
               A    S
               L    T      ⁶L
               I   ⁷G O A L J U D G E
              ⁸L I N E S M A N  E    ¹⁰D  F
               T    N     ¹⁰D   E    W
              ¹¹C E N T E R  E   I    I
               K    T     ¹²R I G H T W I N G
               E        ¹³P E N A L T Y K I L L E R
               E                      C  G
               R       ¹⁴R E F E R E E M
                               ¹⁵T R A I N E R
```

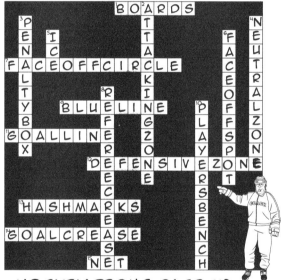

HOCKEY TERMS PAGE 112

```
   O    T   R E B O U N D
   F   ²T   V       I
   F  ³S C R A M B L E V
   S    U   R       E
   I    R  ⁴A S S I S T
   D    N   A       M
   E    O  ⁵S A V E  ⁶L E A D P A S S
        V            E
        E  ⁷F A C E O F F
        R           L
              ⁸B R E A K A W A Y
                    C
            ⁹H A T T R I C K
                    I      H
                    O      E
              ¹⁰I C I N G  C
                           K
```

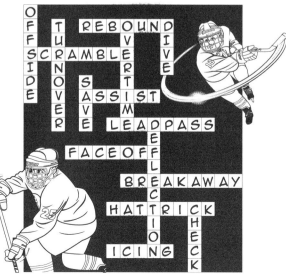

HOCKEY PENALTIES PAGE 132

```
                           ²P
                          ¹E
          ³S L A S H I N G N
              L           A
              B           L
              O           T
             ²R O U G H I N G Y
              W                 ⁵P
            ⁶C H A R G I N G  ⁸H E
              N          ⁷I   I  N
             ⁷B          N   G  A
            ⁹S H O R T H A N D E D
              A          E   H  T
            ¹¹S P E A R I N G    Y
              D          F  ¹²B E N C H M I N O R
            ¹³H O O K I N G R      O   X
              N          E   ¹⁴H O L D I N G
              G          N       C
                        ¹⁵C R O S S C H E C K I N G
```

170